THE SAS
TRACKING & NAVIGATION
HANDBOOK

Also Available from The Lyons Press:

THE **SAS**
TRACKING & NAVIGATION
HANDBOOK

NEIL WILSON

THE LYONS PRESS

GUILFORD, CONNECTICUT

AN IMPRINT OF THE GLOBE PEQUOT PRESS

First Lyons Press edition, 2002
Copyright © 2002 by Amber Books Ltd

The Lyons Press is an imprint of The Globe Pequot Press.

Editorial and design by:
Amber Books Ltd
Bradley's Close
74–77 White Lion Street
London N1 9PF

Project Editor: Chris Stone
Design: Graham Curd
Illustrations: Tony Randell, Patrick Mulrey

Printed in Italy by Eurolitho S.p.A.

2   4   6   8   10   9   7   5   3   1

The Library of Congress Cataloging-in-Publication Data is available on file.

ISBN 1-58574-460-3

Neither the author nor the publisher can accept any responsibility for any loss, injury, or damage caused as a result of the use of the survival techniques used in this book, nor for any prosecutions or proceedings brought or instituted against any person or body that may result from using the aforementioned survival techniques.

Contents

Introduction

This book is for everyone who needs to find their way around the great outdoors. Whether your passion is hiking, climbing, mountain biking, sailing, canoeing or watching wildlife, navigation is a fundamental skill that will not only take you to where you want to go, but could even save your life in an emergency situation.

This book also introduces the skills of tracking – the art of following the trail of an animal or human by reading the signs left behind along their path. Learning how to track gives you a deep insight into the world of animals and birds, and attunes your senses to nature in a way that ordinary hiking never can.

The techniques and methods described in these pages range from the earliest dawn of humankind to the last decade of the 20th century. Tracking and stalking must have been perfected by hunters many thousands of years ago, and their ancient skills have been passed down in an unbroken line to the present day. The map and magnetic compass are over two thousand years old, although the use of the compass for navigation did not become widespread until the 13th century. The handheld Global Positioning System (GPS) receiver did not appear until the mid-1990s.

Although modern technology such as GPS may make you think that the old ways of navigating have become obsolete, this is far from being true. Technology enhances navigation, but it can never replace the need for an understanding of how to find your way with map and compass, or of how to read the sun and stars. A GPS receiver with a flat battery will not show you the way home.

Quite apart from the safety aspects of knowing all the different methods for finding your way in the wilderness, there is a deep satisfaction that comes from learning how the earth, sun, moon and stars relate to each other, and how the landscape around you can be represented in intimate detail on a piece of paper folded in your pocket.

This guide will reveal the secrets of navigating from nature, of fixing your position using map and compass, and of finding your way to a favourite fishing hole using a GPS receiver. Whatever your reason for venturing into the wilds, learning the skills described in this book will make sure you can find your way back again.

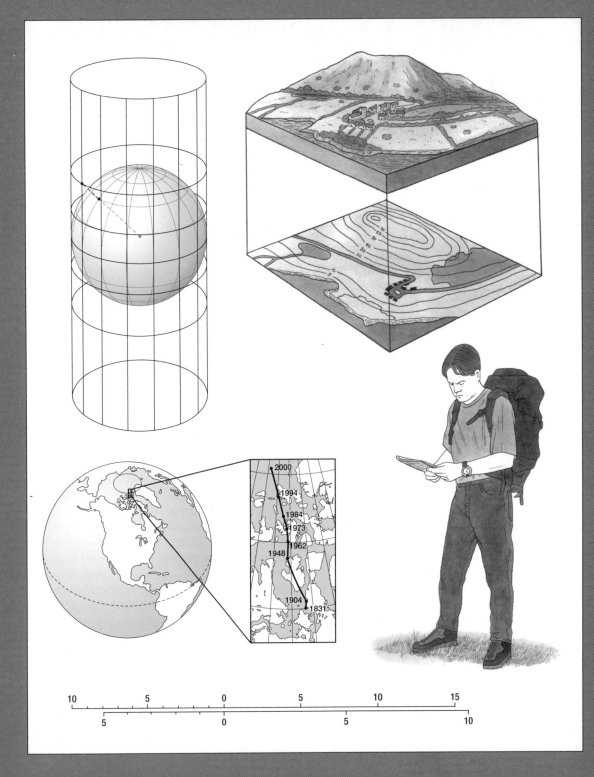

CHAPTER ONE

Maps and Charts

As a navigator, your most important tool is your map. Maps and charts vary in size and detail, but they are the only practical way of finding your destination. So, in order to be able to navigate accurately and safely, you will need to learn the language of maps.

Try this simple experiment. Take a piece of paper and draw a plan of your bedroom, or some other familiar room, as if looking down on it from above. Show where the major features – door, windows and various pieces of furniture – are in relation to each other.

Most people are able to do this easily for places which they know well – their house, their garden, their neighbourhood, even their own town centre. This is because we all carry maps around in our heads. These mental maps record the spatial relationships between the various places we deal with every day, allowing us to find our way to work or to the shops without ever having to look at a street map or ask for directions.

This basic human ability allowed our ancestors to remember where the best hunting was at different times of year, where the most abundant fruit trees grew, where the best fishing was to be found, and how to find their way between these various places. Later, it allowed people to begin exploring beyond their home territory, and to pass on the knowledge they had gained to their fellow tribe members and their children.

The earliest navigators carried all their information in their head, and passed it on by word of mouth. Many people today still do, from Bedouin Arabs and Amazonian tribes-

The cylindrical projection

The cylindrical projection transforms the spherical surface of the earth into a cylinder, which can be 'unrolled' to form a flat, rectangular map.

people to farmers, fishermen and national park rangers. But for most of us, when it comes to exploring the great outdoors – whether on foot or on ski, or by bike, canoe or boat – a map is essential if we are to reach our intended destination and avoid getting lost.

FROM PLANET TO PAPER

Maps have a long history. The earliest surviving representation of a town plan is a wall painting found at Çatal Höyük in Turkey, which dates from around 6200 BC. It was the ancient Greeks, however, who laid the foundations of modern cartography – the first map of the world is thought to have been drawn by the Greek philosopher Anaximander of Miletus in the early part of the 6th century BC.

The ancient Greeks were well aware that the earth was round, having observed its curved shadow during lunar eclipses, and watched ships appear and disappear over the horizon. The Greek astronomer Eratosthenes famously calculated the size of the earth in the 3rd century BC, and the geographer and mathematician Ptolemy published the first *Guide to Geography* in the 2nd century AD, complete with places listed according to latitude and longitude.

The earliest map makers were really editors, collecting descriptions of various parts of the known world from mariners, soldiers and adventurers, and compiling them into a single map. Modern maps are produced using a mixture of land surveys, aerial photographs and satellite imagery.

MAP PROJECTIONS

One of the problems that confronted early map makers was how to accurately represent the curved surface of the earth on the flat surface of a map. The 16th-century Flemish cartographer Gerardus Mercator [Gerhard Kremer (whose surname latinized is Mercator)] solved this problem using what is called a cylindrical projection.

The Mercator projection

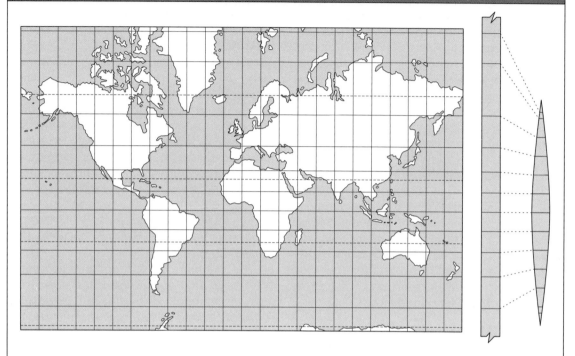

The Mercator projection is a variation of the cylindrical projection, and forms the basis of most maps and nautical charts. A line of constant bearing, such as a compass course, can be drawn as a straight line on a Mercator projection map.

The cylindrical projection

Imagine a transparent globe of the earth, with lines of latitude and longitude and the outlines of the continents marked on it in black, and with a lamp at its centre. Then, imagine a flat piece of paper wrapped around this globe, and touching it only along the equator, in the shape of a cylinder. Switch on the lamp, and the lines on the globe are projected onto the cylindrical screen of the paper – this is known in cartography as a cylindrical projection (see opposite).

The Mercator projection

Gerardus Mercator used a variation of the cylindrical projection for a map of the world that he published in 1569. This showed the meridians of longitude as evenly spaced vertical lines, with the parallels of latitude as horizontal lines, spaced farther and farther apart with increasing distance from the equator. The exact spacing was derived mathematically, so as to maintain an accurate ratio of latitude to longitude.

The unique advantage of Mercator's projection, as far as navigators were concerned, was that any line of constant bearing – for example, a compass course from one place to another – could be drawn on a Mercator map as a straight line. Its great disadvantage was that it expanded and distorted areas in the higher latitudes (more than 60° N and S), and could not represent the circumpolar areas at all. A Mercator map of the world (see page 11) shows Antarctica as a long, straggling landmass along its southern edge, and makes Greenland look as if it is similar in size to South America, whereas it is actually closer in size to western Europe.

Despite these limitations, the Mercator projection is still widely used today for nautical charts, because of the ease of plotting bearings and courses as straight lines.

The Transverse Mercator projection

A modern variation of Mercator's projection, called the Transverse Mercator projection, is commonly used for maps of individual countries, and for the topographic maps used by hikers and mountaineers. In this case, the cylinder that is used as a basis for the projection touches the globe around a specified meridian rather than the equator.

KINDS OF MAPS

There are hundreds of different types of maps, from geological maps and land use surveys to population maps and public transport maps, but there are three main kinds used for navigation in the great outdoors.

Planimetric maps

A planimetric map – from the Latin words *planus* (flat) and *metrum* (measure) – represents the area it covers as a flat surface. It does not include any information on the shape of the landscape, marking only things such as roads, railways, trails, rivers, lakes, towns and villages. Most road maps are planimetric maps.

Topographic maps

Much more useful to the navigator is the topographic map – from the Greek *topos* (a place) and *graphein* (to write) – which provides a detailed representation of the surface features of the area it covers, including hills, valleys, gorges, rivers, lakes, cliffs, forests and marshes, as well as roads, trails, towns and villages. Most maps used for hiking and mountaineering are topographic maps.

Bathymetric maps

More commonly called a chart, a bathymetric map – from the Greek words *bathus* (deep) and *metron* (measure) – is used for navigating at sea or on large lakes (see opposite). It shows the underwater topography, depths of water and dangerous features, such as shallow rocks or wrecks. It also depicts navigational aids, such as buoys and lighthouses, along with details of tidal streams and currents.

MAP MAKERS

The most accurate maps are usually produced by national government agencies using aerial photography and satellite images (see page 14 for National map and chart agencies). Regularly updated, especially in more populated areas, these maps show the year of original publication in the legend, along with the dates of any minor revisions.

Nautical charts are usually produced by separate agencies. The bathymetric data are updated less often, because of the difficulty and expense of surveying the sea floor. Charts of busy coastal areas are kept well up to date, but some of the less-visited parts of the world's oceans have not been resurveyed since the British Royal Navy first charted them in the 19th century.

POSITION

Navigators need a way of specifying a unique position on a map so that it cannot be confused with any other. This is normally carried out by quoting a pair of coordinates that refer to two intersecting axes. The oldest and most familiar system of coordinates is that of latitude and longitude, but there are others, including the Universal Transverse Mercator grid.

Many different coordinate systems have been developed for different purposes, but as a navigator in the great outdoors you will

Nautical chart

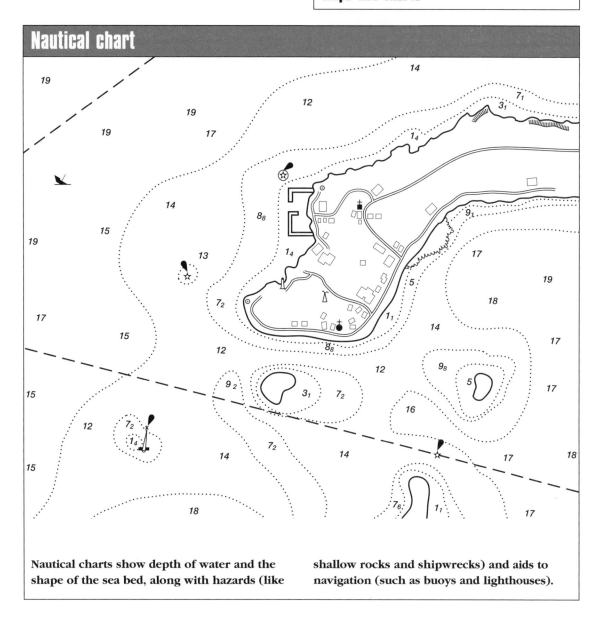

Nautical charts show depth of water and the shape of the sea bed, along with hazards (like shallow rocks and shipwrecks) and aids to navigation (such as buoys and lighthouses).

need to be familiar with only two of these – latitude and longitude, and grid references.

LATITUDE AND LONGITUDE

The traditional way of describing position is by using latitude and longitude. The 2nd-century BC Greek astronomer Hipparchus is credited with the idea of defining posi-tion on a map of the world by drawing a series of parallel, evenly spaced lines paral-lel to the equator, intersected at 90° by a second set of evenly spaced lines. The great geographer Ptolemy, in the 2nd century AD, used latitude and longitude (from the Latin words for breadth and length) to record the positions of the various places described

National map and chart agencies around the world

Topographic maps

Australia: Australian Surveying & Land Information Group (AUSLIG) PO Box 2, Belconnen ACT 2616
Tel: 1 800 800 173
www. auslig.gov.au

Canada: Centre for Topographic Information (CTI) Natural Resources Canada, 130 Bentley St, Nepean, Ontario K2E 6T9
Tel: 613-952 7000;
www.maps.nrcan.gc.ca

France: Institut Géographique National (IGN) 136 bis, rue de Grenelle, 75700 Paris
Tel: 01.43.98.80.00
www.ign.fr

Germany: Bundesamt für Kartographie und Geodäsie (bkg) Richard-Strauss-Allee 11, D-60598 Frankfurt-am-Main
Tel: 0 69-63331
www.ifag.de

Ireland: Ordnance Survey Ireland (OSI) Customer Services, Ordnance Survey Ireland, Phoenix Park, Dublin 8
Tel: 01-802 5300
www.irlgov.ie/osi

New Zealand: National Topographic/Hydrographic Authority (NTHA) Land Information New Zealand, Private Box 5501, Wellington.

Tel: 04-498 9691
www.linz.govt.nz

UK & Northern Ireland: Ordnance Survey (OS) Customer Information, Romsey Rd, Southampton SO16 4GU
Tel: 08456-050505
www.ordsvy.gov.uk

Ordnance Survey Northern Ireland (OSNI). Colby House, Stranmillis Court, Belfast BT9 5BJ.
Tel: 02890-255755
www.osni.gov.uk

USA: United States Geological Survey (USGS). USGS National Center, 12201 Sunrise Valley Drive, Reston VA 20192.
Tel: 1-888-275 8747
www.usgs.gov

Nautical charts

Australia: Australian Hydrographic Service. Locked Bag 8801, South Coast Mail Centre NSW 2521.
Tel: 02-4221 8500
www.hydro.gov.au

Canada: Canadian Hydrographic Service (CHS). 615 Booth St, Ottawa, Ontario K1A 0E6.
Tel 613-995 5249
www.chs-shc.dfo-mpo.gc.ca

France: Service Hydrographique et Océanographique de la Marine (SHOM). BP 30316, 29603 Brest CEDEX.
Tel: 02.98.22.15.84
www.shom.fr

Germany: Bundesamt für Seeschiffahrt und Hydrographie (BSH). Bernhard-Nocht-Strasse 78, 20359 Hamburg.
Tel: 0 40-31900
www.bsh.de

New Zealand: National Topographic/Hydrographic Authority (NTHA). Land Information New Zealand, Private Box 5501, Wellington.
Tel: 04-498 9691
www.linz.govt.nz

UK & Northern Ireland: United Kingdom Hydrographic Office (UKHO). Admiralty Way, Taunton, Somerset TA1 2DN.
Tel: 01823-337900 ext 3342
www.hydro.gov.uk

USA: National Ocean Service (NOS). SSMC4, 13th floor, 1305 East West Highway, Silver Spring, Maryland 20910.
Tel: 301-713 3070
www.nos.noaa.gov

The prime meridian

Although the equator provides a natural baseline for the measurement of latitude, there is no obvious equivalent when it comes to measuring longitude. Ptolemy, in the 2nd century AD, used the 'Blessed Isles' (known as the Canary Islands) – which he thought to be the most westerly point of the inhabitable world – as his prime meridian. However, during the great era of exploration following the discovery of the New World by Columbus in 1492, almost every nation adopted its own, separate prime meridian.

By the 19th century, the predominance of the British Royal Navy in patrolling and charting the world's oceans had led to the widespread use of London as the zero point for measuring longitude, but by 1881 the French and Spanish were still measuring from Paris and Cadiz respectively, and there were at least a dozen different prime meridians in use.

It was not until the International Meridian Conference, held in Washington DC in 1884, that the meridian 'passing through the centre of the transit instrument at the Observatory of Greenwich' in London was adopted as the worldwide standard for 0° longitude.

in his famous work, *Guide to Geography*.

On a globe of the world, the lines of latitude - traditionally called parallels - run around the earth as circles parallel to the equator, diminishing in size as they get closer to the poles. The lines of longitude - known as meridians - run vertically through the poles and intersect the equator at right angles, dividing the earth into a series of segments.

Latitude

Imagine two lines drawn from the centre of the earth, one through your location, and the other through the equator directly to your north or south - the angle between them is your latitude.

Latitude is therefore a measure of how far north or south of the equator you are, expressed in degrees of arc. The latitude of the equator is 0°, and the latitude of the geographic poles is 90° N and 90° S. The latitudes of various cities include:

Reykjavik, Iceland: 64° 09' N
Moscow, Russia: 55° 45' N
Washington DC, USA: 38° 53' N

Kuala Lumpur, Malaysia: 3° 10' N
Buenos Aires, Argentina: 34° 36' S
Wellington, New Zealand: 41° 18'S

Longitude

Longitude is a measure of how far east or west you are of the prime meridian, also known as the Greenwich meridian - a line joining the north and south geographic poles and passing through Greenwich in London, in the United Kingdom. It is the angle between two lines drawn from the centre of the earth, one passing through the equator at the prime meridian, and the other through a point on the equator directly north or south of your position.

The maximum value for longitude is 180°, on the opposite side of the globe from London. The 180° meridian is also the International Date Line, the east side of which is one day earlier than on the west. The longitudes of various cities include:

Honolulu, USA: 157° 51' W
Mexico City, Mexico: 99° 09' W
Paris, France: 2° 20' E

Latitude and longitude

When giving positions using latitude and longitude, the latitude is always given first. For example, the position of Tashkent, Kyrgyzstan is Lat 41° 20' N, Long 69° 18' E.

Latitude and longitude are measured in degrees of arc. Latitude can range from 0° at the equator to a maximum of 90° N or 90° S at the poles. Longitude can range from 0° at the prime meridian to a maximum of 180° east or west.

There are 60 minutes (abbreviated to 60') in one

degree, and 60 seconds (abbreviated to 60") in one minute. One minute of latitude is equal to one nautical mile (about 1.15 imperial miles). The dis-

tance represented by a minute of longitude varies from zero at the poles to one nautical mile at the equator.

Precise positions are given in degrees, minutes and seconds (one second of latitude equals about 30m or 100ft). More approximate positions are quoted in degrees and minutes only, that is, to the nearest nautical mile. When navigating at sea, it is common practice to quote positions to the nearest tenth of a minute, using decimal notation, e.g. 56° 15.7' N, 7° 28.9' W.

Delhi, India: 77° 12' E
Brisbane, Australia: 153° 02' E
Suva, Fiji: 178° 25' E

GRID REFERENCES

Projecting the earth's curved, three-dimensional surface onto a flat, two-dimensional map results in a certain amount of distortion. Modern maps use a mathematical treatment to deal with this distortion, so that important properties – such as distance and area – are portrayed as accurately as possible. However, this treatment often results in the lines of latitude and longitude on the map appearing curved rather than straight.

Because it is inconvenient to use curved reference lines for pinpointing positions on a map, cartographers have developed various systems for superimposing a regular grid onto such maps. The grid consists of two sets of straight, parallel and evenly spaced lines intersecting at

right angles. Each line is specified by a unique number, or combination of letters and numbers, and the whole grid is designed so that the grid reference, or grid coordinates, of any location on the map can be translated accurately into latitude and longitude and vice versa.

In everyday wilderness navigation, it is more common to use abbreviated grid references than the more cumbersome latitude and longitude. Grid references can be quickly and easily read from the map by eye, and a location can be specified – with a precision of 100m (328ft) – as a sequence of just six digits.

Grid references are useful for recording the position of a favourite camp site or fishing spot, and are also used by the emergency services for specifying the location of a casualty during rescue operations. If you ever have to call out the rescue services, the first task is to work out the grid reference of the accident location.

UNIVERSAL TRANSVERSE MERCATOR (UTM) GRID

The USA's former Defense Mapping Agency (now known as the National Imagery and Mapping Agency, or NIMA) developed a special grid system for military use. Known as the Universal Transverse Mercator (UTM) grid, it covers the entire globe with lines spaced at a distance of 1000m (3282ft).

The UTM grid system divides the globe into 60 numbered zones (like narrow segments of an orange), each extending from the north to the south pole and covering 6° of longitude. Zone 1 stretches from the International Date Line (180° W) to 174° W, Zone 2 from 174° W to 168° W, and so on to Zone 60, from 174° E to the International Date Line.

A north–south meridian through the centre of each zone is given a value of 500,000m. The eastings of a point is measured in reference to this line; points to the west of it have values lower than 500,000, points to the east have values greater than 500,000. Northings are measured in relation to the equator, which has a value of zero.

The UTM grid allows precision to the level of a one-metre square. The full UTM grid reference of a specific point on the earth's surface includes the Zone number, then the eastings – distance (in metres) – that the point lies east of the western edge of the Zone, followed by its distance north or south of the equator.

For example, the full UTM grid reference of a point in central New York city is: Zone

---

Getting your bearings

When quoting a grid reference, eastings are given first, then northings This can be slightly confusing, as it is the other way round when using latitude and longitude, where latitude (the equivalent of northings) comes first. If it helps, just remember that E comes before N in the alphabet.

Giving a six-figure grid reference

Find your position on the map, and then find the nearest north–south grid line to its left (west). The number of this line provides the first two digits of your eastings. Estimate the distance between the grid line and your position in tenths of a kilometre/mile

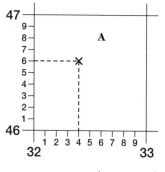

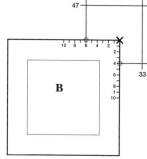

(that is, tenths of the distance between two adjacent grid lines); this gives you the third digit of your eastings. Repeat the process for northings, finding the nearest grid line below (south) of your position and estimating how far north of this line you are. The full six-digit grid reference specifies your position on that particular map to the nearest 100m (328ft). For example, the grid reference of the 'X' in diagram A is 324466.

Diagram B shows a 'romer' – a square marking often found on compass baseplates – being used to measure a grid reference. In this case, the location of 'X' is at 326464.

18   453924E   4506327N. However, the full reference, which uniquely specifies a 1m square, is rarely required. For most purposes a six-figure grid reference, which specifies a 100m (328ft) square, is sufficiently precise. The New York example reduces to 539063.

The UTM grid is shown on most topographic maps produced in the USA, Canada, France, Germany and Australia. A brief note in one corner should confirm this, along with the Zone number and the way in which the grid is displayed, eg '1000-meter Universal Transverse Mercator grid ticks, Zone 18, shown in blue'. On most US maps, the grid lines are not printed on the map, but are indicated by tick-marks along the margins – these can be joined up using a pen or pencil, or a transparent overlay can be used.

The grid lines are usually numbered in the following manner: 380000mE for eastings, and 4045000mN for northings; the larger figures in bold represent 1km (0.6 mile) intervals. Often, only the corners of the map sheet are marked with the full reference; the intermediate grid lines are numbered with just the two-digit 1km (0.6 mile) markings.

THE UK NATIONAL GRID

During World War II, the Ordnance Survey (or OS, the UK's national mapping agency) introduced its own grid system, known as the National Grid. It is similar to the UTM but it covers only England, Wales and Scotland. It does not extend to Northern Ireland or the Republic of Ireland.

A bird's-eye view

A map is a two-dimensional representation of the earth's surface, as if seen from directly overhead. Contours are used to show the height and shape of the land.

The National Grid is a system of 25 x 100km (62 mile) squares, stretching from the Scilly Isles in the southwest to the Shetland Islands in the northeast. Each one is designated by a pair of letters (from HL in the northwest to TV in the southeast) and contains 100 x 10km squares (62 x 6 mile); each 10km (6 mile) square in turn contains 100 1km (0.6 mile) squares.

All of the OS's 1:50,000 and 1:25,000 maps are overprinted with National Grid lines at 1km (0.6 mile) intervals, making it very easy to read or plot grid references by eye, without the need for a ruler, pencil or overlay.

OTHER GRIDS

Northern Ireland and the Republic of Ireland are covered by a grid system similar to the UK National Grid, but with 20 x 100km (62 mile) squares, each designated by a single letter. All maps of 1:50,000 and larger scale are overprinted with the Irish Grid, and grid references are defined in the same way as with the National Grid. New Zealand also has its own system called the New Zealand Map Grid (NZMG), based on the same principle.

There are other grid systems that you may come across, especially if you use a GPS receiver (see Chapter Six). These include the US Military Grid Reference System (MGRS), which is based on the UTM grid; the Universal Polar Stereographic (UPS) grid, used in the polar regions; and the Maidenhead grid system used by amateur radio operators. However, these are of little practical use to most hikers and sailors.

THE LANGUAGE OF MAPS

A map is simply a representation of some part of the earth's surface, reduced to two dimensions. Think of it as a picture of the landscape as seen from a helicopter hovering directly overhead, with the natural features, roads and buildings represented by colours and symbols. An experienced navigator can look at a map and see in his mind's eye the landscape it represents.

In order to become a proficient navigator, you will need to learn the language of maps, and as with any language, it takes practice to become fluent. Don't wait until you are out in the great outdoors before starting to learn – buy some topographic maps of an area you are interested in (or borrow them from a public library), and study them at home. In time you will be able to read a map as easily as you read a book.

There are three fundamental features of a map that you will need to be familiar with.

Typical map scales and their uses

1:10,000 (10cm to 1km, around 6 inches to 1 mile) – city street atlas

1:50,000 (2cm to 1km, around 1 ¼ inches to 1 mile) – topographic hiking map

1:250,000 (1cm to 2.5km, around 1 inch to 4 miles) – regional road map

1:1,000,000 (1cm to 100km, around 1 inch to 16 miles) – national road map

1:75,000,000 (1cm to 750km, around 1 inch to 1200 miles) – map of the world on a double-page spread in an atlas

Units of distance

Metric	*Imperial*	*Nautical*
100 centimetres (cm) = 1 metre (m)	12 inches = 1 foot (ft)	6ft = 1 fathom
1000m = 1 kilometre (km)	36 inches = 3ft = 1 yard (yd)	608ft = 1 cable
1km = 0.621 miles = 0.540 nm	5280ft = 1760 yd = 1 mile	6080ft = 10 cables = 1 nautical
	1 mile = 1.609km = 0.869nm	mile (nm)
		1nm = 1.151 miles = 1.852km

Bar scales

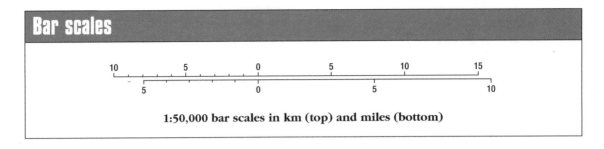

1:50,000 bar scales in km (top) and miles (bottom)

These are the scale, the north point, and the legend.

SCALE

Every map should have a scale, which tells you the relationship between a distance on the map and the corresponding distance in the real world. The scale is usually shown both as a representative fraction and as a bar scale.

REPRESENTATIVE FRACTIONS

A representative fraction (eg 1:50,000) shows the relationship between a distance

Nautical chart margins

The eastern and western margins of nautical charts are divided into minutes and tenths of a minute of latitude. As one minute of latitude is equal to one nautical mile, these graduated margins can be used as a convenient bar scale for measuring distances on the chart.

measured on the map and the corresponding distance in the real world. For example, on a 1:50,000 map, one unit of measurement on the map equals 50,000 units in the real world. Put another way, the map represents the real world at 1/50,000th of its actual size.

Thus 1cm on a 1:50,000 map represents 50,000cm (ie 500m, or half a kilometre) on the ground. And 1 inch is equivalent to 50,000 inches (ie 4167ft, or 1389 yards, or about ⅘ mile).

BAR SCALES

A bar scale is simply a bar, or line, marked off in units of distance (usually kilometres or miles). You can measure the distance between two points on the map using dividers (or by laying the edge of a piece of paper between the points and marking the distance with a pencil), then transferring this to the bar scale and reading off the distance.

NAUTICAL CHARTS

The margins of nautical charts are marked in degrees and minutes of latitude and longitude, allowing positions to be read and plotted easily. The east and west margins, which show latitude, also double as a handy bar scale in which one minute of latitude equals one nautical mile.

MEASURING DISTANCES ON MAPS

There are various ways of measuring distances on a map. For straight-line distances, you can use a ruler, and convert the distance in centimetres into kilometres or miles using the representative scale (eg 12cm on a 1:50,000 map would be 6km, or 9 ½ miles on the ground). Or simply use a couple of pencil marks on the edge of a piece of paper to transfer the distance to the bar scale.

For measuring distance along a twisting course – for example, the route of a winding road, river or trail – you will need another method. The easiest way is to use a map measurer (see Chapter Two), but you can also use a piece of string, copper wire or dental floss laid along the route, and then compared to the bar scale or a ruler. Both of these methods rarely manage to account for every twist and turn in the route, and it is best to add 10 per cent to the distance obtained.

If your map has a 1km (0.6 mile) grid, the simplest method of all – and one which has

the advantage of needing no instruments or other aids – is just to estimate the distance by counting grid squares. Remember that the diagonal distance across a 1km (0.6 mile) grid square is about 1.4km (0.9 mile).

NORTH POINT

Every map needs a north point, so that it can be properly oriented in relation to the real world, and so that bearings can be accurately plotted on it and read from it. Most maps have three different north points – true north, magnetic north and grid north (see below).

Traditionally, true north is indicated on a map by a line ending in a star, magnetic north is shown by an arrow and/or the letters MN, and grid north by a cross and/or GN.

On nautical charts using the Mercator projection, the top of the chart points to true north (there is no grid north). Compass roses are printed on the chart in several places – the outer ring shows bearings in relation to true north, the inner ring in relation to magnetic north.

True north

True north is simply the direction of the earth's geographic north pole – the northern end of the planet's axis of rotation – a point that is fixed and unchanging. The meridians of longitude on a map or chart are aligned with the direction of true north.

Magnetic north

Although true north is the ultimate geographical reference point, it is not much use to a navigator with a compass that points to magnetic north. The difference

North point

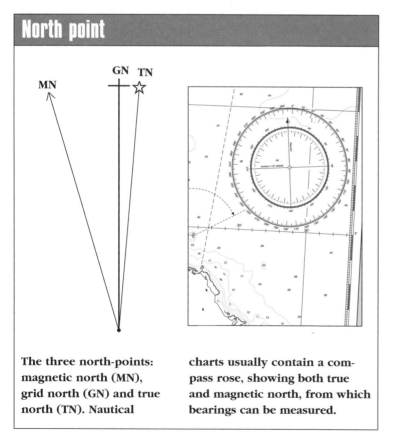

The three north-points: magnetic north (MN), grid north (GN) and true north (TN). Nautical charts usually contain a compass rose, showing both true and magnetic north, from which bearings can be measured.

between magnetic north and true north is called magnetic declination (see Chapter Two). Declination varies with geographical position and with time, so a map must show not only the value of declination at the time of its publication, but also how it changes with time. This is usually written on the map in the following form:

'The direction of magnetic north is estimated at 4° 22' west of grid north in July 2000. Annual change is about 13' east.'

So if you were to use this map in the year 2004, you would assume that the declination had decreased by 52', making it 3° 30' (ie 3.5°) west.

Grid north

Most maps used by hikers are overprinted with a grid (see the previous section Position – Grid references), aligned with the edges of the map. The top ends of the vertical grid lines therefore represent grid north. Just to make things more complicated, this

is rarely the same as either true north or magnetic north. The difference in bearing between true north and grid north usually amounts to no more than one or two degrees. However, for most wilderness navigation using map and compass, you can forget about true north – grid north and magnetic north are all you need.

Grid north is important because it allows you to orientate your map easily using a baseplate compass, and simplifies the process of plotting and reading compass bearings (see Chapter Three – Navigation techniques).

LEGEND

The map legend is the descriptive information that appears in the margin of a map. It includes the title, sheet number, scale, the north points, and a lot of other useful information, including the year the map was printed and revised. It also contains an explanatory list of the symbols used to represent various natural and man-made features.

MAP SYMBOLS

The colours and symbols used on a map vary from one country to another, and even from one map series to another. Familiarize yourself thoroughly with the map series you intend to use most often.

Some features are fairly standard. The sea, lakes, canals, rivers and streams are usually shown in blue, and forests and woodland are green. Contour lines are most often marked in brown or orange. Main roads are often shown in red, and railways as black lines. Trails and footpaths are commonly

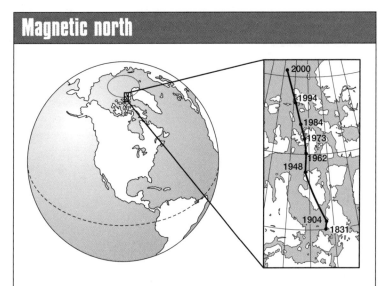

Magnetic north

The location of the north magnetic pole has changed over the course of time. In the last 100 years it has drifted slowly north by around 960km (600 miles).

Map detail

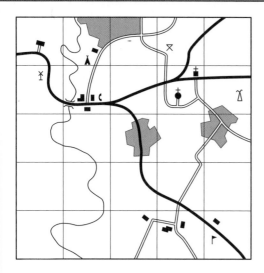

Maps use a standard set of symbols to represent objects in the real world, such as roads, towns, buildings and so on.

indicated by a broken black or red line.

Some map series may show extra information for tourists; for example, the Ordnance Survey 1:50,000 maps (in the UK) mark the locations of tourist information centres, nature reserves, car parks, cycle routes, long-distance footpaths, camp sites, public telephones and major tourist attractions.

Most topographic maps include a complete list of symbols – sometimes called the map key – in the legend. A notable exception is the USGS series of maps, which have a limited range of symbols actually printed on the map. The full range is described in a separate, free pamphlet called *Topographic Map Symbols*.

Nautical charts also rely on a separate booklet to list all the symbols and abbreviations used.

You should be aware that features such as roads and buildings are rarely shown exactly to scale. In order to improve clarity and readability, things are usually shown slightly oversize. For example, a road that is 15m (49ft) wide in real life would be only 0.3mm (0.013in) wide on a 1:50,000 map. To improve legibility, the road will actually be drawn about 1mm (0.039in) wide. However, the centre line of the road, and the centre point of any building, will be plotted accurately.

THE SHAPE OF THE LAND

The most important skill you will develop while learning the language of maps is the art of interpreting the shape of the land. Topographic maps depict the variations in the height and form of the landscape using a combination of spot heights and contours.

In the past, surveyors went out in teams and laboriously measured the height of every feature using theodolites, levels and staffs. Today, contours are usually plotted using stereoscopic aerial photographs and satellite imagery.

SPOT HEIGHTS

In cartography, the height of any place above sea level is called its elevation. Maps show

Typical map symbols

♯	Church with tower	⌣	Bridge
♦	Church with spire	⌐	Golf course
▛	Building	Å	Camp site
✾	Built-up area	✕	Picnic area
▬	Main road	△	Triangulation pillar
⌇	Minor road	⟊	Windmill or water pump
⌇	Stream	Å	Radio mast
ℂ	Public telephone	P	Post office

the elevations of the top of hills and mountains using spot heights – normally a simple black dot or x with the height in metres beside it. Spot heights are also shown at other places, often along main roads.

In many places the spot height is accompanied by a surveyor's mark – either a triangulation point (marked on the map by a small triangle) or a bench mark (symbolized by the letters 'BM'). A triangulation point (often shortened to 'trig point') is often marked on the ground by a small concrete pillar with a metal fitting on top (for surveying instruments); a bench mark is usually marked by a small metal plaque or stud. If you come across either of these in the field you will know your exact elevation – useful if you want to check your altimeter (see Chapter Two).

MAP OR CHART DATUM

All the elevations on a topographic map are measured above a specified zero point, known as the vertical map datum; this is normally mean sea level (the average level of the sea, between high and low tide).

Nautical charts show the depth of water measured below chart datum; this is usually the lowest astronomical tide (LAT) – the lowest point that the tide will ever fall to.

Make use of your map

When you are learning how to navigate, refer to your map as often as possible. Orient it correctly and identify as many natural and man-made features as you can, until you are as comfortable reading a map as you are reading a newspaper.

CONTOURS

Although spot heights provide useful information, contours are far more important to the wilderness navigator. Contours are imaginary lines that join up points of equal elevation, and in so doing reveal the actual shapes of hills, valleys, ridges, plateaux, peaks and plains.

CONTOUR INTERVAL

The difference in height between one contour and the next is called the contour interval. This varies from map to map - you can find the actual value by looking at the map legend. A typical contour interval for USGS 1:24,000 maps is 20ft; Canadian 1:50,000 maps typically use 50ft intervals, and UK Ordnance Survey 1:50,000 maps use 10m intervals.

Usually every fourth or fifth contour is marked with a heavier line and labelled with its elevation. These are called index contours. The printed elevation is shown so that you can check which index contour is higher in areas where the direction of slope - uphill or downhill - is not immediately obvious.

The contour interval is important, because any landscape features smaller than it may not show up on the map. For example, an 8m (26ft) cliff might not be visible on a map with a 10m (33ft) contour interval, but if you walk over an 8m (26ft) cliff you will certainly know about it.

GRADIENT

The steepness of a slope is called its gradient, and it is usually expressed as the ratio of vertical to horizontal distance. For example, if you were walking up a slope with a 1 in 10 gradient, you would gain 1m (3ft) in height for every 10m (33ft) you travelled horizontally.

Contours show the gradient of a slope by their spacing - a gentle slope has widely spaced contours, a steep slope has closely spaced contours. At a vertical cliff, the contours all merge into a single line.

You can calculate the gradient of a slope by measuring the horizontal distance (H) between two contour lines, and dividing it by their vertical separation (V) - using the same units for each measurement. For example, if you measure the distance between the 200m and 400m contours on a 1:50,000 map and find it to be 2cm (ie 1km, or 1000m), then H/V = 1000/200 = 5, meaning that the gradient is 1 in 5.

Gradient can also be expressed as the angle between the slope and the horizontal (inverse tangent V/H), and as a percentage (V/H x 100), where a flat surface is 0 per cent, a 1 in 1 slope is 100 per cent, and a 1 in 5 slope is 20 per cent. Typical gradients and slope angles are listed in the box below:

The art of reading the landscape using contours is fully explained in Chapter Five.

Calculating gradients

1 in 10	6°	10 per cent	easy walking
1 in 5	11°	20 per cent	an average hill-path; a steep hill on a motor road
1 in 4	14°	25 per cent	a steep trail; about the steepest hill you will come across on a motor road
1 in 3	18°	33 per cent	a strenuous climb
1 in 2	27°	50 per cent	very steep and strenuous slope; there will probably be steps and switchbacks on the trail
1 in 1	45°	100 per cent	extremely steep scrambling; you will need to use your hands as well as your feet

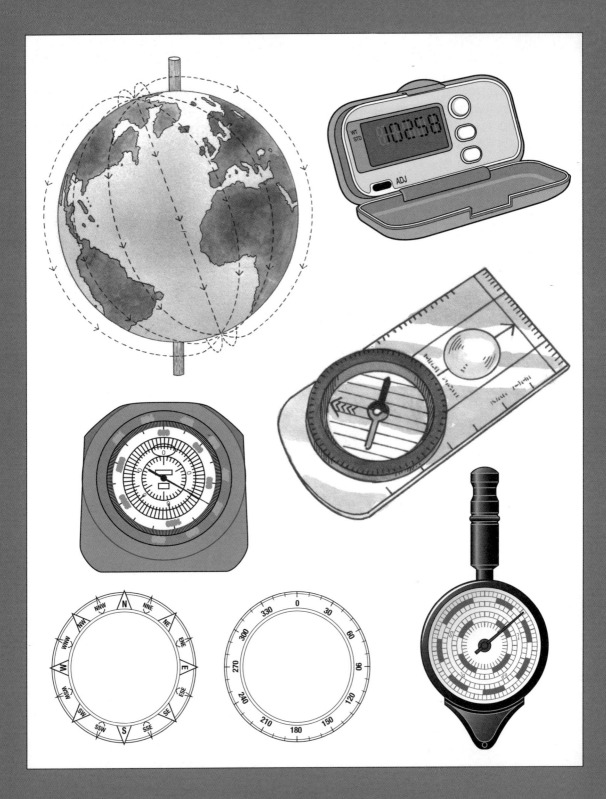

CHAPTER TWO

Compasses and Instruments

Although it is possible, in an emergency, to navigate without the aid of a compass – or, indeed, any other instruments – all navigators need to know how to use a compass. Other useful gadgets include altimeters, pedometers and map measurers.

Most of the time you will not need a compass, or any other instrument, to keep track of your position. A good map, an observant eye and frequent checking of your progress against the map should mean that you are always fairly certain of your position. Nevertheless, you should never venture into the wilds without a compass. In mist, cloud or darkness, in unfamiliar or featureless terrain, or at sea, it is an essential navigational tool.

COMPASSES

No one is certain when the magnetic compass was first invented, but there are written sources which suggest that the Chinese were using primitive magnetic compasses as long ago as the 1st century AD.

The use of the magnetic compass spread from China to Europe along the trade routes of the Silk Road in the 11th and 12th centuries, and by the 13th century its use for navigation at sea became widespread.

Although gyroscopic and electronic compasses have now largely replaced magnetic ones on military and commercial shipping, magnetic compasses are still routinely used by fishermen, recreational sailors, canoeists, kayakers, hikers and mountaineers.

Bar magnet

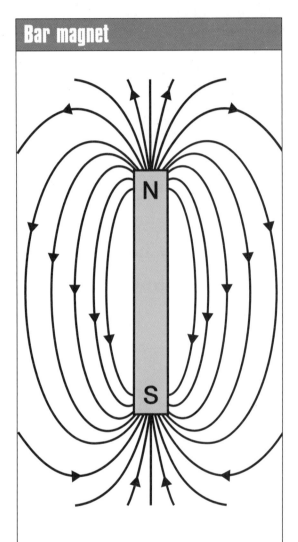

The lines of force in the magnetic field surrounding a simple bar magnet run parallel to the magnet's N–S axis. A compass needle would align itself parallel to these lines.

WHAT DOES A COMPASS DO?

Most important to note is the fact that a compass does not point towards true north, the direction of the geographic north pole (see Chapter One). It points to the magnetic north pole, which is presently located in the Arctic islands of northern Canada.

As an added complication, the earth's magnetic pole does not remain in the same place – it is constantly in motion (see boxed text, The wandering pole). Fortunately for navigators, it moves slowly and predictably.

THE EARTH'S MAGNETIC FIELD

You might recall school science experiments where you sprinkled iron filings on a sheet of paper with a bar magnet held underneath. The filings lined up with the magnetic field to produce a pattern similar to that shown in the illustration, left.

The earth has a magnetic field caused by convection currents flowing within its core of molten iron. You can imagine the field as if there were a giant bar magnet hidden inside the planet. However, the north pole of this magnet occupies a different position from the geographic north pole (see right).

A compass needle is quite simply a piece of magnetized steel that behaves much like one of the iron filings in the bar magnet experiment. When it is allowed to rotate freely, the needle aligns itself with the earth's magnetic field.

INCLINATION

The lines of force in the earth's magnetic field are not everywhere parallel to the earth's surface. The closer you get to the north and south magnetic poles, the more steeply inclined the lines of force become – this effect is called inclination. This means that in the regions close to the magnetic poles, a freely suspended compass needle will point down at an angle to the horizontal. The closer to the pole, the steeper the angle. In theory, if you were standing directly

The earth's magnetic field

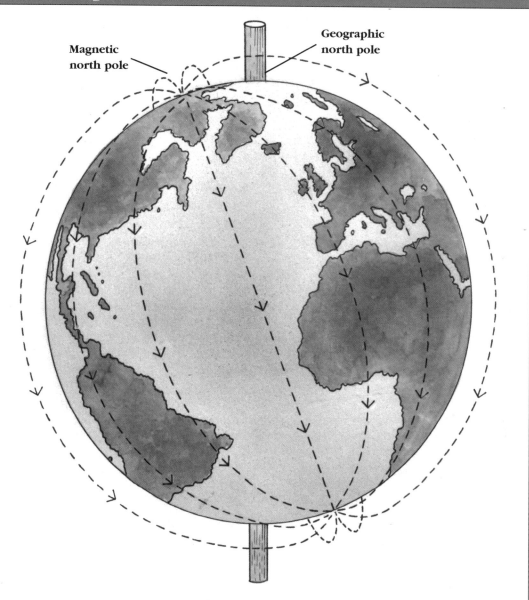

Magnetic north pole

Geographic north pole

The earth's magnetic field behaves as if there was a giant bar magnet inside the planet, with its north pole located in northern Canada. A compass needle will align itself with the lines of magnetic force, running in straight lines between the north and south magnetic poles, so that the 'north' end of the needle points towards the north magnetic pole. This is unlike the geographic north pole, shown here at the north end of the earth's axis of rotation.

The wandering pole

The earth's magnetic poles are not fixed, but move slowly with time. A scientific expedition determined that the location of the north magnetic pole in 2000 was at Lat 79° 19' N, Long 105° 26' W, on the Isachsen Peninsula of Ellef Ringnes Island in the far north of Canada. The illustration demonstrates how the magnetic pole has drifted slowly northward throughout the 20th century.

over the magnetic pole, a compass needle would point vertically downward.

Compass manufacturers compensate for this tendency by counterweighting their compass needles to balance out the effect of inclination. For this purpose, the world is divided into five zones – magnetic north, north magnetic equatorial, magnetic equatorial, south magnetic equatorial and magnetic south. The magnetic north zone includes all of North America, Europe, Siberia, Central Asia, China and Japan. The magnetic south zone includes Australia and New Zealand.

Compasses are best suited for use only in the zone for which they were manufactured. Trying to use one in another zone – for example, using a North American compass in Australia – may result in the needle tilting and dragging against the housing so badly that it will not give an accurate reading.

POINTS OF THE COMPASS

Early mariners marked their compasses with what are known as the cardinal points – north (N), south (S), east (E) and west (W) –

and the intercardinal points – northeast (NE), southeast (SE), southwest (SW) and northwest (NW) – which subdivided the compass card into segments of 45°.

There are smaller subdivisions, such as north-northeast (NNE), east-northeast (ENE), east-southeast (ESE), south-southeast (SSE) and so on. Smaller subdivisions exist,

Compass bearings

Compass bearings: points of the compass vs degrees

N	↑	000°
NE	↗	045°
E	→	090°
SE	↘	135°
S	↓	180°
SW	↙	225°
W	←	270°
NW	↖	315°

Compass markings

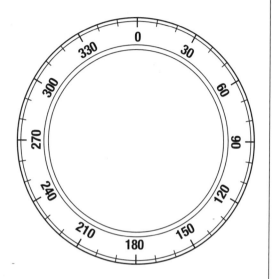

Early compasses were marked with the 'points' of the compass: north (N), north–northeast (NNE), northeast (NE) and so

on. Modern compasses usually have a graduated scale divided into 360 degrees, with the value marked every 10, 20 or 30 degrees.

such as north by east (NxE), which is halfway between N and NNE, and northeast by north (NExN), which is halfway between NNE and NE. Altogether there are 32 points of the compass, each separated by 11.25°. They are rarely used these days, except to indicate general directions.

DEGREES

Modern compasses are graduated in degrees, from 000° to 359°; they also show the cardinal marks N, S, E, and W. Baseplate compasses used by hikers usually have graduation marks every 2° around the dial; prismatic compasses and hand-bearing compasses are more precise, with marks every 1° or even 0.5°. Steering compasses are not used for taking bearings, and have marks every 5°.

Compass bearings and courses measured in degrees are usually expressed as three digits, even if the value is less than 100°. For example, east is 090° (oh-nine-oh degrees) and northeast is 045° (oh-four-five degrees).

MAGNETIC DECLINATION

The difference in bearing between true north (the direction of the geographic north pole) and magnetic north at any given place is called the 'declination' for that location. (Note that on nautical charts it is called 'variation', because the term declination has a different meaning, used in astro-navigation).

Magnetic declination varies with place and with time. The values of declination for a particular year can be plotted on a map called an isogonic chart (see overleaf). Declination is described as so many degrees east or west, depending on whether the compass points to the east or west of true north.

Magnetic declination

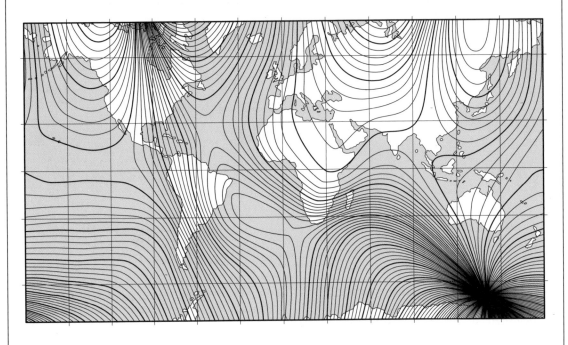

Magnetic declination (also called magnetic variation on nautical charts) is the difference in bearing between true north and magnetic north, measured in degrees. An isogonic chart shows how declination varies around the world at a particular time. The isogonic lines connect places with equal values of declination.

TYPES OF COMPASS

A modern magnetic compass is basically a very simple instrument. It consists of a magnetized needle, with one end coloured (usually red) to indicate north, mounted on a pin on which it can rotate. Good quality compasses usually have several refinements, including a fluid-filled chamber to dampen the movement of the needle, a balanced needle that compensates for inclination, and a jewel bearing to reduce friction as the needle rotates. There are many different kinds of compass, designed to meet the needs of different users, from hikers and sailors to soldiers and surveyors.

Baseplate compass

The baseplate compass is the kind most commonly used by hikers and mountaineers. It was invented in Sweden in the 1920s for the sport of orienteering, and is also known as an orienteering compass or protractor compass.

In its most basic form, the compass consists of a circular, fluid-filled capsule, mounted on a transparent, rectangular baseplate. It is constructed so that the capsule – which contains the compass needle – can be rotated relative to the baseplate.

The capsule has a graduated dial, marked around its circumference with the cardinal points N, S, E and W, and divided into degrees, and its transparent base is marked with an orienting arrow, flanked by a series of parallel orienting lines. The baseplate usually has an arrow indicating direction of travel, and may have other features, including rulers and a magnifier.

More sophisticated models may have a lid with a mirror and sight, which makes it easier to measure precise compass bearings of landmarks. Other features may include an adjustable declination scale (to automatically correct for declination), and a clinometer (for measuring angles of slope).

Adjustable compasses have a tiny screw in the dial which allows you to adjust the orienting arrow in the capsule to east or west. If you set this equal to the declination for the area you are travelling in, then you do not have to make any further corrections for declination when transferring bearings between map and compass. However, you will have to remember to adjust the setting when you visit an area with a different declination. Chapter Three describes how to use a baseplate compass for practical navigation.

Prismatic compass

Prismatic compasses are designed for taking precise bearings, and are generally used only by surveyors and soldiers. They are heavier and more solidly built (often of brass or bronze) than baseplate compasses, and have front and rear hairline sights for aiming at distant objects. They also have a prism which allows you to read the bearing off the compass card while looking through the sights.

Types of compass

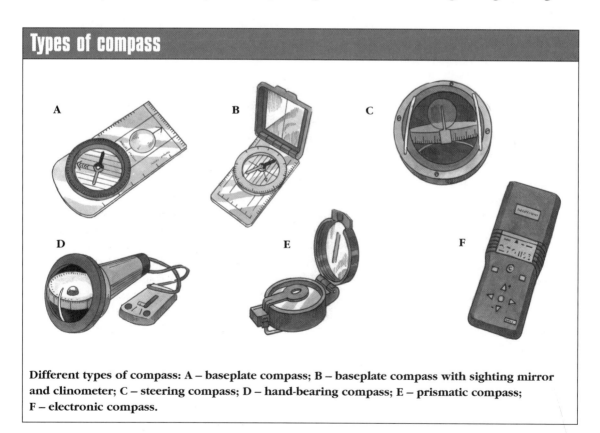

Different types of compass: A – baseplate compass; B – baseplate compass with sighting mirror and clinometer; C – steering compass; D – hand-bearing compass; E – prismatic compass; F – electronic compass.

While capable of taking very precise bearings – down to 0.5° – a prismatic compass is less convenient than a baseplate compass for most wilderness navigation, as you will also need to carry a ruler and protractor for transferring bearings to and from the map.

Steering compass

A steering compass is used on a boat to steer an accurate compass course. It is usually fixed to a bulkhead, or mounted in a binnacle, where the helmsman can see it clearly.

Steering compasses are card compasses. This means that direction is indicated by a freely rotating, circular card, which has one or more compass needles fixed to its lower surface. The card itself is marked in degrees, and has a turned-down edge which can be read either from above, or from behind.

The lubber line is a vertical marker aligned exactly fore and aft so that it indicates the boat's heading. To steer a compass course, the helmsman swings the boat's head around until the lubber line lines up with the desired heading on the compass card.

You can buy small steering compasses that are suitable for mounting on the spraydeck of a sea kayak, or the thwart of a canoe or sailing dinghy.

Hand-bearing compass

A hand-bearing compass is the nautical equivalent of a prismatic compass. As the name suggests, it is designed for taking bearings of objects for the purpose of fixing your position at sea – a boat's steering compass is not usually suitable for taking bearings.

You hold the compass up at eye level and line up the sights on the object of interest, then read the bearing from the compass card. Some models can be mounted on a bracket in your boat and double as a steering compass.

Electronic compass

In recent years, electronic compasses have become widely available and relatively inexpensive. An electronic compass contains a sensor that detects the earth's magnetic field direction, and provides a digital or analog readout of your heading or of the bearing of an object. They can also store bearings and routes in memory, and usually include an electronic clock and timer.

They suffer from the same disadvantage as prismatic compasses in that you cannot use them to measure or plot bearings directly on the map, and as they run on batteries – which can go flat – they cannot be relied on in emergency situations.

An electronic compass may be worth considering, however, if you want to mount a steering compass in a car or truck. A digital compass can be adjusted much more easily and effectively to allow for the magnetic effect of the vehicle's steel body.

DEVIATION

Remember that a compass needle is very sensitive, and can be deflected by magnets, electrical currents and objects made of iron or steel. Any deflection of a compass needle away from magnetic north is called deviation.

When using a compass, make sure it is kept at least a few feet away from objects that might cause deviation – cameras, flashlights, radios, ice axes, knives and rifles are all good examples. Less obvious objects to be aware of include battery-powered wristwatches, stainless steel watch straps, metal belt buckles and steel-framed spectacles. Also, do not use a compass near power lines, pipelines, railroads or automobiles.

There are also certain parts of the world where natural magnetism can cause a compass to give an erroneous reading, or even render it useless. The mineral magnetite (an oxide of iron) is the magnetic lodestone that ancient navigators first used to magnetize their compass needles. It is found in certain igneous rocks, and can occasionally occur in concentrations large enough to deflect a

Correcting for declination

In order to transfer a bearing from compass to map, you will have to correct it for declination. The rule is that, from compass to map, you subtract westerly declination from, and add easterly declination to, the bearing as measured with the compass. Make sure that you use the correct declination – for true north or grid north (see Chapter One) – depending on the map or chart you are using.

For example, if the declination is 5° W, and you have measured the compass bearing of a mountain peak as 132°, then the bearing to plot on the map will be 127°.

If the declination is 12° E and the compass bearing is 355°, then the bearing to plot on the map will be 007°.

From map to compass, it works the other way round – you add westerly declination to, and subtract easterly declination from, the map bearing to get the compass bearing.

If this sounds confusing, fortunately there's a useful phrase that may help you to remember: 'Empty sea? Add water'. This reminds you that from map to compass (MTC = 'empty sea'), you add westerly declination (add W = 'add water'). From this starting point, you can work out the rest of the rule.

---

compass needle. These areas are said to have local magnetic anomalies.

Magnetic anomalies are usually marked on the maps or charts where they occur. Some popular hiking areas that suffer from magnetic anomalies include Mount Hale in New Hampshire and the Ramapo Mountains in New Jersey (USA); around Georgian Bay on Lake Huron, and north of Kingston, Ontario (Canada); and the Cuillin Hills on the Isle of Skye (UK).

Checking for deviation

It is always a good idea to check your compass for deviation before setting out on a long trip. Do this wearing your backpack and other equipment that you would carry when navigating.

From a known location – a hilltop is ideal – use the map to measure accurate bearings to three or four distant landmarks evenly spaced around the horizon. Then use your compass to measure the same bearings, correct them for declination, and compare them to the map. If they are out by more than three degrees or so, start thinking about what you are carrying that might be causing the deviation.

Steering compass deviation

A boat's steering compass should always be checked for deviation after it has been fitted, and again after any new electrical equipment or a new engine has been installed. From a known position, swing the boat's head around until it points to landmarks of known bearing, and then check the compass reading (corrected for declination).

In this case, you draw up a deviation card, which shows the effect of deviation at different headings. If the deviation is greater than 1° or 2°, then it is applied as a correction (in the same way as declination) when translating bearings between chart and compass.

ALTIMETERS

An altimeter measures altitude, or height above sea level. Atmospheric pressure decreases with height, and an altimeter works simply by measuring pressure.

Knowing your exact altitude can be very useful when navigating in the mountains in poor visibility. For example, if you are climbing upward in thick mist and reach a summit, can you be sure you are at the actual summit of the mountain or at a subsidiary summit? An altimeter will tell you. This can be very important when the only safe route off the summit requires you to follow a compass course – if you follow this course from the wrong summit, you could end up in trouble.

Alternatively, if you are descending a mountain ridge in poor visibility, and your route means you must drop down to one side of the ridge to avoid a cliff or steep drop, an altimeter can tell you when you have reached the correct height.

Because atmospheric pressure is also affected by weather systems, an altimeter must be checked frequently and reset to the correct height, whenever you are at a point of known elevation – sea level, for example, or at any point on the map that has an accurate height.

Take into account the weather conditions when using an altimeter. In stormy weather, when atmospheric pressure is changing relatively rapidly, an altimeter must be reset as often as possible, and may become unreliable within an hour or two of being adjusted. In fine, settled, anticyclonic conditions, when atmospheric pressure is relatively steady, an altimeter will be more reliable and will need adjusting less often.

WRISTWATCH ALTIMETERS

Altimeters used to be bulky, expensive instruments that were used only by surveyors and Himalayan mountaineers, but in recent years lightweight wristwatch altimeters have come onto the market at very reasonable prices. Many are multipurpose instruments that include barometer and electronic compass functions too.

Because an altimeter measures atmospheric pressure, it can also serve as a barometer. If it is kept at a constant elevation – for example, at base camp, or on a boat – it can monitor and record changes in pressure caused by weather systems, and serve as a useful weather forecasting tool.

Even overnight changes can provide a clue to what the weather might be doing. If you wake up in the morning and your altimeter shows that the altitude of your camp has mysteriously increased during the night, this means that the atmospheric pressure is falling – usually a sign of bad weather. Rising pressure – indicated by a decrease in the altitude reading overnight – often heralds a period of settled weather.

MEASURING SPEED AND DISTANCE

Keeping track of the distance you have covered is an important part of the navigational technique known as dead reckoning (see Chapter Three).

There are two ways to keep track of distance covered. One is to measure it directly, by using a pedometer or by mentally counting paces. The other is to know the speed you are travelling over the ground, and measure the time taken.

PEDOMETERS

A pedometer (see page 38) is an instrument that records the number of paces you make while you are walking – you wear it on a belt at your hip and a motion sensor counts your paces. Once you have calibrated it to your own stride length, it can display the distance you have walked in any units you choose. Coupled with an electronic timer, it can also calculate your average speed.

The problem with pedometers is that they only work accurately on relatively level, easy-going terrain where you can maintain a constant stride length. If you are walking slowly uphill, running downhill, climbing over obstacles, scrambling down scree or hacking through jungle, it becomes much less effective.

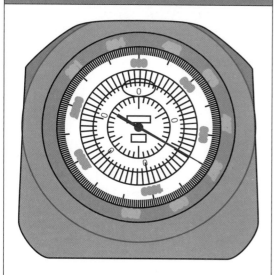

Altimeter

An altimeter measures altitude by detecting changes in atmospheric pressure. As the pressure can also be affected by changing weather conditions, an altimeter should be checked and reset whenever you reach a point of known altitude.

However, it is often on flat and featureless terrain – ground ideally suited to a pedometer – that you will need to measure distance most accurately.

PACING

Pacing is the low-tech alternative to using a pedometer – you simply count your own paces instead of employing an electronic instrument to do it for you.

As with a pedometer, pacing requires calibration. The best way is to set up a measured distance – for example, 100m or 100yds – and walk it repeatedly, wearing your normal hiking gear and backpack, counting paces as you go. This should give you the average number of paces it takes you to cover the distance.

Again, as with a pedometer, this technique will only measure distance effectively on relatively level, uncluttered ground. However, with plenty of practice over a set distance, you can make your calibration method work on different kinds of terrain too.

One potential problem with pacing is keeping an accurate count of your paces. Do not count every single pace, count double paces – for example, count every time your right foot hits the ground. Some hikers pick up a handful of pebbles, and place one in their right hand every time the count reaches 100; others keep track with an inexpensive, plastic tally-counter.

If you are in a group, the person who is pacing can shout out 'one hundred' every time their count reaches 100, and a second person can take on the task of keeping track of the number of hundreds called out.

CYCLE COMPUTERS

There is a vast range of cycle computers available for touring cycles and mountain bikes. All of them will accurately record your average speed and distance travelled. A cycle computer works by counting the revolutions of the bike's front wheel – you attach a tiny magnet to the spokes of the wheel, and a sensor mounted on the forks detects every time it passes.

Having calibrated the computer to the circumference of the wheel, it provides a remarkably accurate readout of speed and distance, and is not subject to the vagaries of terrain suffered by pedometers.

LOGS

A log is a nautical instrument that measures speed and distance travelled at sea. Distance travelled at sea is almost always calculated by measuring speed, and multiplying it by time. If your boat is moving at 4 knots, then you know that after four hours it will have travelled 30km (16 nautical miles) through the water.

Pedometer

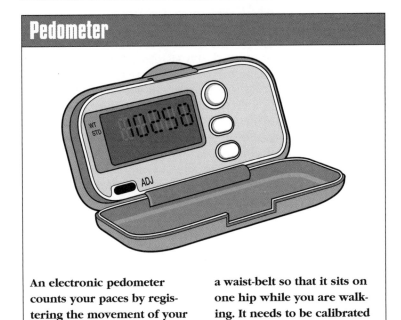

An electronic pedometer counts your paces by registering the movement of your body. It is usually attached by a waist-belt so that it sits on one hip while you are walking. It needs to be calibrated to the length of your stride.

Kayakers and canoeists rarely use instruments of any kind to measure speed. They learn through experience what their cruising speed is in various conditions, and how it is affected by headwinds and following winds.

Even small-boat sailors travelling along the coast rarely have the need to measure speed or distance, as most of their navigation is done by pilotage (reference to landmarks) and distance covered can be read off the chart. It is only when out of sight of land, or in poor visibility, that the ability to measure speed and distance becomes important to them.

The simplest speedometer for a boat is the so-called chip log (see boxed text, Using a basic chip log). More sophisticated electronic logs suitable for small boats are of two types – towed and hull-mounted.

A towed log consists of an impeller, which rotates as it is towed behind the boat, and a deck unit which reads impulses from the impeller and displays a readout of speed and distance.

Hull-mounted logs work in the same way, except that the impeller is a small paddle-wheel which projects into the water beneath the boat through a small opening in the hull.

SEXTANTS

A sextant is a complex, expensive, bulky and heavy instrument that is unlikely to be carried by anyone other than sailors on transoceanic voyages and members of scientific expeditions to remote areas. It is used for astro-navigation – the art and science of finding your position using a sextant, the sun and the stars.

In the past, a sextant was necessary to fix your position when navigating out of sight of land, or in any area that lacked good, accurate maps. The advent of handheld GPS receivers (see Chapter Six) has rendered the sextant almost redundant. GPS receivers are smaller, lighter, cheaper, more accurate, easier to use, and will work in overcast conditions when the sun and stars are not visible. On the other hand, a sextant requires no batteries, and is often carried on ocean-cruising yachts as a reliable backup to the GPS.

The function of a sextant is simply to measure precisely the angle between yourself and two distant features using mirrors. The instrument features a graduated arc of 60°. Usually, the distant features are the sun (or a star) and the horizon. Such measurements allow you to work out your latitude and longitude.

Anyone interested in a full treatment of astro-navigation should consult *Celestial*

Navigation in a Nutshell by Roy T. Maloney and *Reed's Sextant Simplified* by D. Pike.

OTHER EQUIPMENT

It is possible to navigate safely and successfully using nothing but a map and compass, but there are various other extra pieces of equipment that may prove very useful.

MAP CASE

A map case is nothing more than a tough, waterproof nylon pouch with a clear PVC window for your map - folded so that your area of travel is visible - to protect it from rain and mud. Most have a strap or cord so that you can hang it round your neck, and pockets for compass and pencil. An inexpensive alternative is to use a clear plastic bag, big enough to hold the folded map.

PENCIL, ERASER AND NOTEBOOK

A pencil is needed for plotting your position on a map or chart, and for drawing courses and bearings. In order not to damage the paper, and so that lines can be easily erased, a soft pencil is best - a 2B lead pencil is ideal. Carry one or two spares, depending on the length of your trip, and bring along a penknife to keep it sharp. A soft eraser may also be useful. A small notebook is not necessary for day hikes, unless you enjoy keeping a journal, but it comes in handy for noting down compass bearings when fixing your position, and for keeping track of time and distance covered when navigating in unfamiliar areas.

WATCH

An accurate watch is a very handy navigational tool. It is useful for keeping track of your progress, and judging whether you are on schedule to make your next camp before nightfall. It may also help with navigating in poor visibility to measure how far you have travelled at a given speed. In an emergency, it can be used as an aid for finding direction (see Chapter Four).

FLASHLIGHT

Never travel without a flashlight, even on a day hike. If you suffer an accident or get lost in poor visibility, you may find yourself having to navigate in darkness. A light will enable you to read your map, walk safely on a boulder-strewn trail - hiking in the dark without a torch can be almost impossible -

Sextant

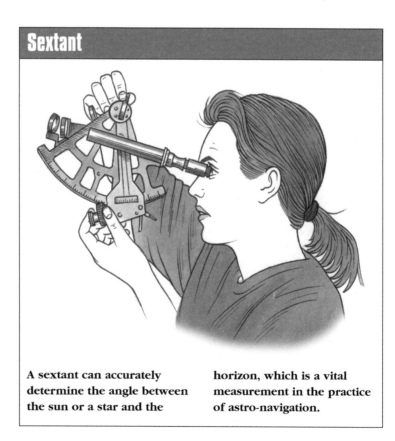

A sextant can accurately determine the angle between the sun or a star and the horizon, which is a vital measurement in the practice of astro-navigation.

Using a basic chip log

You can easily make a basic chip log from a piece of wood (or the 'chip') and some line, and use it to measure the speed of your boat. You need a line that is exactly 50ft (15.24m) in length from the chip to the loop in your hand, and a watch (or just count the seconds in your head).

Toss the log into the water ahead of you, but fairly close to the side of the boat (A). Start timing when the chip passes directly abeam, ie at 90° to the boat's heading (B),

and stop when you feel it tug on the line (C).

The following table gives your boat speed (in knots, or nautical miles per hour) for various timings:

30 sec	1 knot
15 sec	2 knots
10 sec	3 knots
7.5 sec	4 knots
6 sec	5 knots
5 sec	6 knots

and to signal to rescuers in the event of an emergency (see Chapter Eight).

A head-torch, which leaves your hands free to hold map and compass, or to steady yourself while climbing over obstacles, is so useful that there is little point considering any other kind of flashlight as your first choice. Always carry at least one set of spare batteries, and two spare bulbs. On a long trip, always make sure you carry a spare torch.

MAP MEASURER

A map measurer is a handy little tool. It has a small, ridged wheel on its base, which you run along your proposed route on the map and the dial displays the total distance in miles and/or kilometres. Most have dials graduated for 1:25,000, 1:50,000 and 1:100,000 scale maps. Use it at home, during the planning stage, as there is no need to carry one with you on your hike.

A cheaper and simpler alternative is to lay a length of string along your route, following all the twists and turns, and mark its length with a pen, then measure the string with a ruler or against the map's bar scale.

CHART INSTRUMENTS

The traditional instruments used by marine navigators were the parallel rule and dividers. A parallel rule consists of two straight-edge rulers linked by pivoted metal arms; these enable it to be 'walked' across a chart, transferring a bearing from a compass rose (see Chapter One) to any other place on the chart. Dividers are used for measuring distances on the chart.

If sailing a small boat, kayak or canoe, a Douglas protractor is more convenient and less expensive. This is simply a piece of transparent plastic, 12.7cm (5in) square, marked with intersecting horizontal and vertical grid lines and graduated in degrees all round the edge, from 000° to 359°. It serves as a combined ruler and protractor, and is used in much the same way as the baseplate of a baseplate compass (see Types of compass, above) to quickly read and plot bearings on the chart.

Map measurer

This handy tool can easily and quickly measure distance along a twisting road or trail marked on the map. It has a range of graduations for use on maps of different scales.

The Roman mile

Roman soldiers used to count double paces while marching along the roads that crisscrossed the Roman Empire. The English word 'mile' is derived from the Latin *mille passus* (a thousand paces), the measure of distance used on Roman roads. The original Roman mile was 1475m (4840ft), making the average Roman soldier's double pace just under 1.5m (5ft). This is slightly less than the average pace of adult males today.

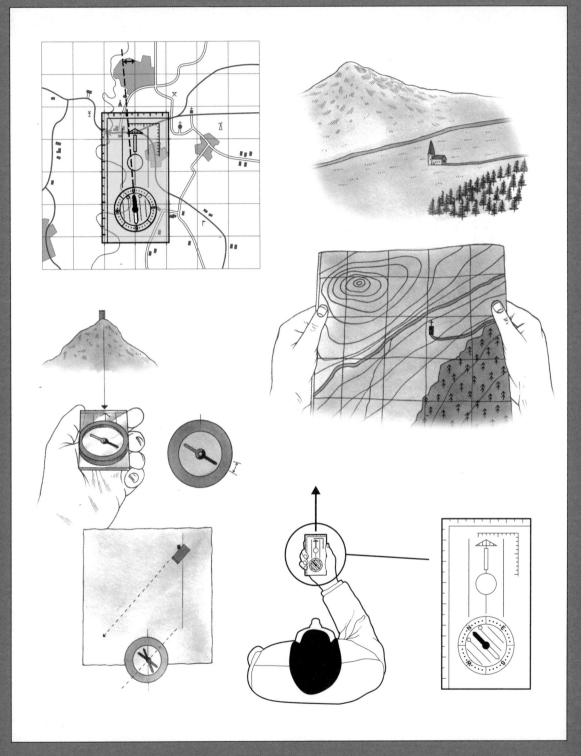

CHAPTER THREE

Basic Navigational Skills

The purpose of learning how to navigate is not to find out where you are when you are lost – it's about not getting lost in the first place. Good navigation is about knowing where you are and where you're going at all times.

The first two chapters covered the fundamental tools of the navigator – maps and compasses. This chapter describes the basic skills you will need to use your map and compass together in the practice of navigation, including setting the map, taking the bearing of a landmark, fixing your position using resection, following a compass course, and using dead reckoning. It also includes information on small-boat navigation in tidal waters.

In addition to the basic skills of navigation using map and compass, you also have the options of 'low-tech' navigation using various clues provided by nature (Chapter Four), and 'high-tech' navigation using a handheld Global Positioning System (GPS) receiver (Chapter Six). However, do not imagine that one of these three methods is somehow superior to any of the others.

So, who needs to know about navigating by the sun and the stars when you have a

Using a compass to set the map

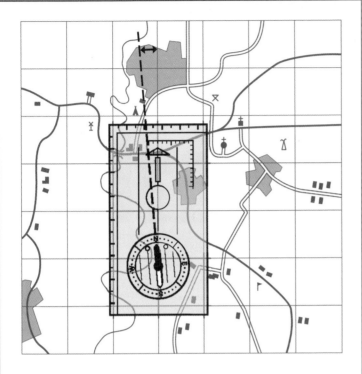

With the compass housing set to the declination between grid and magnetic north, and the direction of travel arrow parallel to the **North–South grid lines, map and compass are rotated together until the compass needle is aligned with the orienting arrow.**

Well, there will be plenty of occasions when the sky is obscured by cloud.

Each method has its strengths and weaknesses, and a good navigator will use all the means and methods at his or her disposal, using one to confirm and back up another. When it comes to knowledge of navigational methods, more is definitely better – and the basic skills described here form the foundation of good navigational practice.

A SENSE OF DIRECTION

When they get lost, people often say that they have no sense of direction. What they really mean, however, is that they were not really paying enough attention to where they were going in the first place.

Developing a sense of direction is simple – it is about taking note of the features and landmarks around you, and being aware of the direction you are travelling in. There is nothing mysterious about it – it is just the simple art of observation. Once you are alert to these things, keeping a mental note of your position and direction of travel becomes second nature.

MAP AND COMPASS

For this section, you will need to be familiar with the various features of a baseplate compass – the baseplate, housing, orienting arrow, orienting lines and the direction of travel arrow. Review the relevant section in Chapter Two, if necessary.

compass in your pocket? The answer is that compasses can be lost or broken, and there are parts of the world where magnetic anomalies can make a compass unreliable.

In theory, you might think you do not need a compass if you have a GPS receiver. But what happens if your receiver's batteries go flat, or you are in terrain where you cannot obtain good satellite reception?

Then again, if you can manage to find your way by the sun and the stars, why bother with a compass or a costly GPS receiver?

ORIENTING YOUR COMPASS

The most basic thing you can do with a compass is to find magnetic north. Rotate the compass housing until the dial reads N (000°). Then hold the compass level and allow the needle to settle (making sure there are no metal objects nearby that might cause an error – see Chapter Two). The red end of the needle points to magnetic north.

If you now rotate the entire compass so that the needle is aligned with the orienting arrow, the direction of travel arrow will be pointing towards magnetic north.

FINDING TRUE NORTH

To find true north using a baseplate compass, first rotate the compass housing so that north on the dial lies over the index mark for the direction of travel arrow. Then, adjust for declination as you would when converting a bearing from compass to map (by adding west, or subtracting east declination). For example, if declination is 10° W, set the dial to 010°; if declination is 15° E, set the dial to 345°.

Next, rotate the whole compass until the north (red) end of the compass needle is aligned with the orienting arrow. The direction of travel arrow will now be pointing to true north.

FINDING GRID NORTH

Finding grid north uses exactly the same procedure as for true north, except that the declination correction should be made using the difference between magnetic north and grid north. This is usually slightly different from the declination between magnetic and true north – you can find the appropriate value in the map legend (see Chapter One).

SETTING THE MAP

You will find that a map is much easier to read if it is oriented so that it is aligned with the features on the ground, with its north-point pointed towards true north. This is called setting the map, and there are two ways to go about it – using the compass, and using landmarks.

USING THE COMPASS

To set a map using the compass, follow the basic procedure described above for finding true or grid north. After making the adjustment for declination, lay the compass on the map, with the long edges of the baseplate parallel to the grid lines, and the direction of travel arrow pointing towards the north edge of the map. Now rotate the map and compass together until the north (red) end of the compass needle is aligned with the orienting arrow. Your map is now properly aligned with the landscape.

USING LANDMARKS

While navigating, you should be keeping track of where you are by consulting your map frequently. Remain aware of the landmarks and landscape features around you, and how they are plotted on the map.

To set the map using landmarks, simply identify a prominent object or feature ahead of you (its compass direction is not important), and rotate the map in your hands so that an imaginary line between your position and the object on the map points toward the feature in the real world (see the church in the illustration on page 46).

When a map is properly set, you can then identify other features on the map and in the landscape in their proper relation to each other. For example, in the illustration, the hill is behind and to the left of the church both on the map and in the view you are looking at.

If the direction in which you are facing is anything other than due north, of course, you will find yourself holding the map sideways, at an angle, or even the wrong way round (if you are facing south), but you will soon get used to reading it this way as well.

Using landmarks to set the map

Hold the map in front of you, and rotate it until the landmarks on the map occupy the same relative positions as the landmarks you can see, eg the hill is behind and to the left of the church both in the view and on the map.

Taking the compass bearing of an object

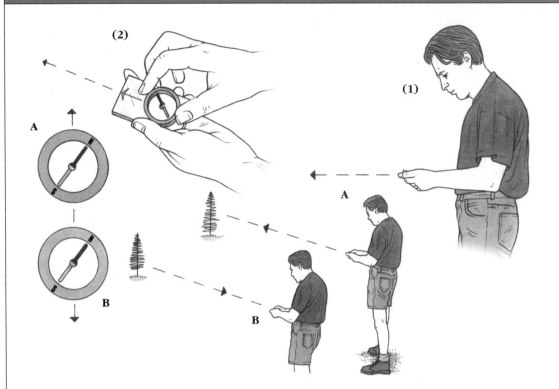

Hold the compass in front of you, and point the direction of travel arrow directly towards the object whose bearing you want to measure (1). Then, rotate the housing until the orientation arrow is aligned with the compass needle

(2) and read off the bearing. For a direct bearing (A), align the N end of the orienting arrow with the N end of the needle. For a back bearing (B), align the N end of the orienting arrow with the S end of the needle.

COMPASS BEARINGS AND POSITION LINES

A bearing is the angular direction of a point, line or course measured in relation to true, grid or magnetic north, and is usually expressed in degrees.

A direct bearing is measured from your position towards an object; a back bearing is measured from the object to your position. A direct bearing and back bearing of the same object obviously differ by 180°.

For example, in the illustration above, the direct bearing from the man to the tree is

320°, and the back bearing from the tree to the man is 140° (320° -140° = 180°).

FROM MAP TO COMPASS

Taking a bearing from the map, and then following the resulting compass course, is the most commonly used procedure in navigation, and one that you should practise until you are completely comfortable with it.

You can use this method whenever you know your position, and want to head

Taking a bearing from the map

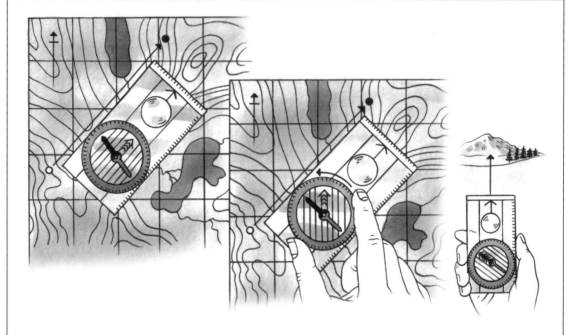

Lay one edge of the compass baseplate along the line that you want to follow, with the direction of travel arrow pointing in the direction you want to go. Rotate the compass housing (ignore the needle) until the orienting lines are parallel to the grid lines. Correct for declination, and the compass is set to show the course to your chosen destination.

towards an objective that is out of sight, or to follow a particular course in order to avoid danger. The classic example is finding your way off the summit of a mountain in poor visibility. You can, however, use it to take the most direct route across a featureless moor or plateau, or to head directly towards a destination obscured by trees or an intervening slope.

● Place the compass on the map, and lay the edge of the baseplate along your desired line of travel, with the direction of travel arrow pointing the way you want to go.
● Rotate the housing so that the orienting lines are parallel to the grid lines on the map, with the N on the dial pointing to the north edge of the map. Ignore the compass needle at this point.
● If necessary, correct the bearing for declination (see Chapter Two) – subtract east declination or add west declination by rotating the dial the appropriate number of degrees clockwise or anticlockwise, respectively. (If you have a compass that has automatic declination adjustment, you can miss out this step.)
● Hold the compass in front of you, with the direction of travel arrow pointing away from you. Turn around until the compass needle is aligned with the orienting arrow, with the NORTH (red) end of the needle

pointing to the NORTH end of the arrow. You are now facing the direction in which you want to travel.

FROM COMPASS TO MAP

To transfer a bearing from the real world to a map, you simply reverse the previous procedure. This method can be used to plot the bearing of a landmark on the map, either to create a position line (see below), or to help identify an unknown landmark.

However, there is one vital difference. What you want to measure is a back bearing (ie the bearing FROM the landmark TO your position).

● Hold the compass in front of you, and point the direction of travel arrow directly at the object or feature whose bearing you wish to take. For greater accuracy, try sighting along one edge of the baseplate.
● Keeping the baseplate steady, rotate the compass housing until the orienting arrow is aligned with the compass needle, but with the NORTH end of the arrow under the SOUTH (white) end of the needle; this gives you a back bearing instead of a direct bearing.
● If necessary, correct the bearing for declination (see Chapter Two) – add east declination or subtract west declination by rotating the dial the appropriate number of degrees anticlockwise or clockwise, respectively. (If you have a compass that has automatic declination adjustment, you can miss out this step.)
● Place the compass on the

map, and lay the edge of the baseplate over the feature whose bearing you have taken – you can now ignore the compass needle. Move the compass until the orienting lines are parallel to the north–south grid lines on the map, and the NORTH end of the orienting arrow is pointing to the north edge of the map.
● Draw a line from the feature towards the direction of travel arrow – this is the back bearing, and your position lies somewhere along this line.

Aligning the south end of the compass needle with the orienting arrow is simply a way of saving you the trouble of measuring the direct bearing of the object and then subtracting 180°.

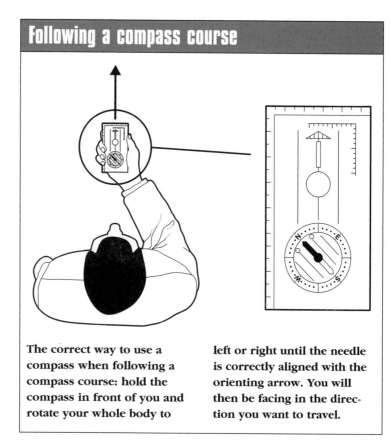

Following a compass course

The correct way to use a compass when following a compass course: hold the compass in front of you and rotate your whole body to left or right until the needle is correctly aligned with the orienting arrow. You will then be facing in the direction you want to travel.

Back bearings

It is important to understand the difference between a direct bearing and a back bearing. The direct bearing of landmark is the compass direction from you to the landmark (A). The back bearing is the direction from the landmark to you (B), and differs from the direct bearing by 180°.

POSITION LINES

Taking a bearing of a mapped object provides you with a position line – you know that your position lies somewhere along that line. A bearing is only one example of a position line – there are many others that you can use. A position line does not need to be straight. It can be curved, irregular or even circular – as long as it can be plotted accurately on the map, it can be used to fix your position.

LINEAR FEATURES

Many position lines do not need any measurement at all – any linear feature that can be identified on the map will do. If you are on a road, trail, river, shoreline or mountain ridge, you already have one position line.

TRANSITS

A transit is simply a straight line drawn through two identifiable points on the map. If you are standing at a point where you can see these two features line up one in front of the other, then you are on a transit. A transit makes an excellent and accurate position line.

In the illustration on page 51, the hiker is on a transit joining the west end of the island and the summit of the mountain behind it. She is also on a trail, which provides a second position line, so she can fix her position on the map at X without having to take a compass bearing.

CIRCULAR POSITION LINES

If you know exactly how far away you are from a mapped object, you can plot a circular position line around it. Ways of estimating your distance from an object include judging distance using hand angles, and judging distance to the horizon (both described in Chapter Four), and using a running fix (see Navigating at sea, later in this chapter).

FIXING YOUR POSITION

In order to fix your position precisely, you need to have at least two intersecting position lines. Two bearings will do, or any combination of the position lines described above. The more accurate the position lines, the more accurate the position.

Anyone who lives in a city probably uses intersecting position lines every day. When you phone a friend and say you're at the corner of Market St and Pitt St, you are defining your position by using two intersecting position lines – in this case, they are both streets. This method of fixing your position using two or more bearings is called resection.

RESECTION WITH TWO BEARINGS

This technique can be used to pinpoint your position when you are in the middle of a featureless area – a moor, a desert plain, a plateau – always provided there are suitable landmarks from which to take bearings.

The method is straightforward. Simply use your compass to record the bearings of two or more landmarks (see the diagram on page 52), correct the bearings for declination, and then plot the bearings on your map. Where the two lines intersect is your position.

The accuracy of a position obtained using resection should take into account any potential sources of error. When you record

A transit

A transit is the extension of a straight line joining two features that you can identify on the map. Keep your eyes open for naturally occurring transits, as they provide excellent position lines.

the bearing of a landmark using an ordinary baseplate compass, it is unlikely that you will be able to measure it more precisely than to the nearest 2°. If you have a more advanced compass with sighting aids, or a prismatic compass, you might be able to read a bearing to the nearest degree.

Resection

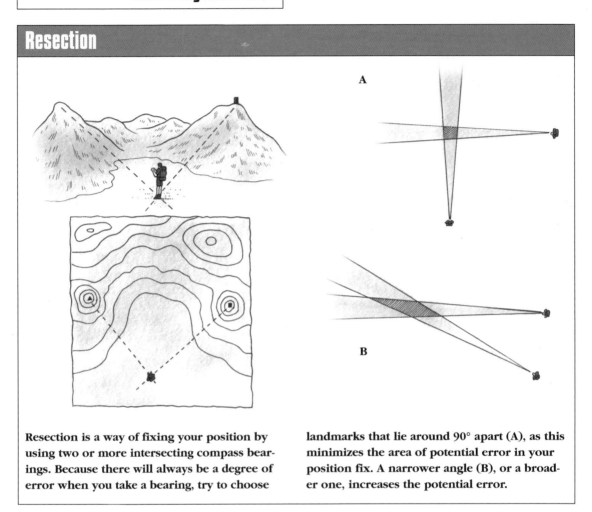

Resection is a way of fixing your position by using two or more intersecting compass bearings. Because there will always be a degree of error when you take a bearing, try to choose landmarks that lie around 90° apart (A), as this minimizes the area of potential error in your position fix. A narrower angle (B), or a broader one, increases the potential error.

An error of 2° in a bearing will introduce an error of around 30m (100ft) for every 1km (0.6 mile) between you and the landmark. For this reason, when choosing landmarks to fix your position it is best to select two objects that are roughly 90° apart, as these will produce a smaller area of potential error than objects that are closer together.

RESECTION WITH THREE BEARINGS

When plotting a position fix using three bearings, it is only rarely that you will find all three lines intersecting in a single point. More commonly, slight errors in reading and plotting the bearing will result in a small triangle, traditionally known as a 'cocked hat' (the expression comes from the triangular hats worn by officers in Britain's Royal Navy in the 18th century).

When a fix produces a cocked hat (see opposite), you would normally take the centre of the triangle to be your position. However, if there are any dangers nearby – such as the rocks, marked by small crosses, on the chart – then you should assume that your position lies on the corner of the triangle that lies closest to the danger ('O' on the diagram). That way, any error in your position is more likely to be on the side away from the danger.

FOLLOWING A COMPASS COURSE

Although measuring a compass course from the map is a fairly straightforward process, following that course accurately across the ground is not so easy. Walking any distance in a straight line is virtually impossible without some landmark to aim for or a compass to guide you. On rough ground, obstacles will deflect you from the straight-line course. Even on smooth and level terrain, small asymmetries in stride length cause most people to veer off course to one side or the other. If you walk far enough, this can result in the old movie cliché of the man lost in the desert for days who stumbles across a line of footprints, only to discover that they are, in fact, his own.

A 'cocked hat'

Errors often result in three compass bearings intersecting in a small triangle (which is known as a 'cocked hat') rather than a single point. Assume your position to be at the corner of the triangle that is nearest to any potential hazard.

WALKING A COURSE

The main purpose of a compass course is to allow you to travel in a straight line towards an objective that is not visible, either because it is obscured by intervening vegetation or landscape features, or because of poor visibility caused by mist, bad weather or darkness.

However, attempting to follow a course by simply staring at the compass held in front of you will just end up with you walking into trees. There are easier ways.

If you have to follow a compass course for any distance, then rather than staring at the compass while you walk, it is easier to break the course up into shorter segments. Choose some intermediate landmark or feature that lies directly in the line of the course indicated by your compass. It might be a boulder, one edge of a patch of trees or bushes, a bend in a river – anything distinctive that will give you something to aim at.

Whatever it is, you can then put away your compass and walk towards your chosen object by the easiest route – which does not have to be a straight line – and when you reach it, you take out your compass again

Maintaining a compass course around an obstacle

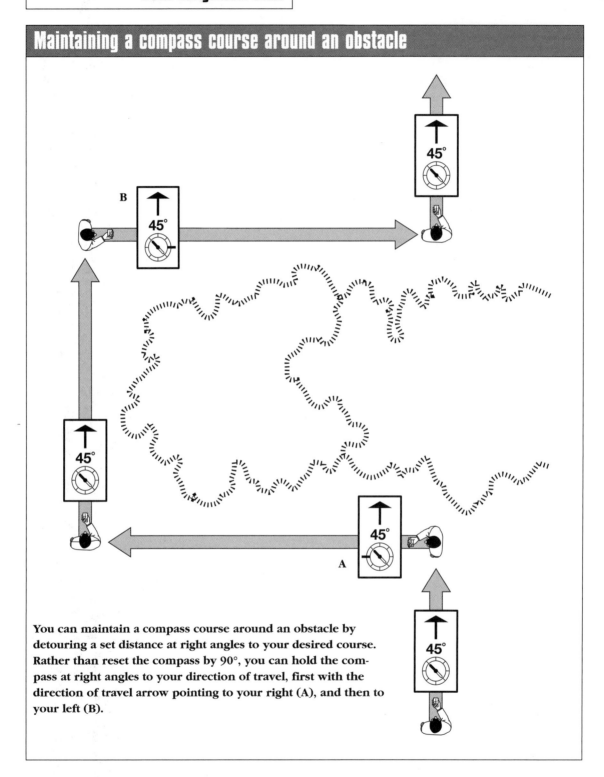

You can maintain a compass course around an obstacle by detouring a set distance at right angles to your desired course. Rather than reset the compass by 90°, you can hold the compass at right angles to your direction of travel, first with the direction of travel arrow pointing to your right (A), and then to your left (B).

and choose another mark up ahead. Repeat this procedure as often as necessary until you reach your chosen destination.

Better still, if visibility allows, choose some mark far in the distance, beyond your destination - such as a notch or a peak on the skyline - and use that to keep a check on your course.

On a clear night, you can choose a prominent star or constellation in the night sky to indicate your desired direction of travel. But remember that the stars move across the sky (see Chapter Four), and you will need to keep checking the compass frequently and, if necessary, change to another star as time passes.

AVOIDING OBSTACLES

While following a compass course you might run into an obstacle that prevents you continuing on a straight line. It might be a boulder field, a swamp, a lake, a cliff, or a river or ravine that can only be forded or crossed further upstream or downstream. How do you get around the obstacle while remaining on your compass course?

Small obstacles

If the obstruction is small enough for you to see the far side of it - for example, a river where the nearest bridge is far downstream - then you can use the method described above for following a course by choosing intermediate landmarks.

Sight across the river to the far bank and choose an intermediate landmark that lies on your desired bearing. Then, head downstream to the bridge, cross it and come back upstream until your chosen landmark becomes visible. Head towards it and continue on your compass course.

Big obstacles

With larger obstacles like hills, cliffs and patches of impenetrable forest, you may not be able to see the far side. In these situations

you will have to detour around the obstacle using the compass.

When you reach the edge of the obstacle, adjust your compass to give a course which lies exactly 90° to the left or right of your desired line of travel. Then use pacing (see Chapter Two) to measure the distance you have travelled to outflank the obstacle. Reset the compass to your original compass course, and continue until you have cleared the obstacle.

Then adjust the compass to 90° on the other side of your desired course, and pace out the same distance that you measured on the first leg of the detour before resuming your original compass course.

NAVIGATING IN POOR VISIBILITY

When your view ahead is obscured by heavy rain, falling snow, fog, dense forest or darkness, then maintaining a compass course by sighting on an intermediate landmark will obviously not be possible. In such conditions, your actions will depend on how important it is to follow your compass course exactly.

If the distance to be covered is short and accuracy is not crucial, then just holding the compass in front of you and checking it occasionally as you walk will be sufficient. You should be able to follow a reasonably accurate course in this manner for up to 800m (0.5 mile) or so.

However, if straying from the exact compass course might be inadvisable or even dangerous - for example, if you are using a compass bearing to avoid the edge of a cliff, or to find a safe ridge descending from a mountain summit - then you can use the method illustrated on page 56.

One member of the party, the leader, (A) sets off in the direction of the compass course while the other (B) remains where he is. The leader goes as far as he can without losing sight of his companion. He then turns around and uses his compass to check that his partner (B) is on the exact back bearing of the compass course – if not, he moves sideways until he is. He then signals his companion (B) to join him before repeating the process as often as needed.

Even if you are travelling alone, you can still use a variation of this method over short distances. Instead of using a companion as a reference point for a back bearing, you can leave behind a backpack or trekking pole to sight on. Of course, having checked your course, you will then have to go back and retrieve it, having first marked your forward position with another marker. As this involves walking each leg three times, you obviously would not want to rely on it to cover long distances.

DEAD RECKONING

There may be times when you have to travel through an area with no visible landmarks, and no other way of obtaining a position fix. This might include travelling in dense forest or jungle, in featureless terrain, in bad weather, in fog or mist, and at sea when out of sight of land.

In order to keep track of your position in such situations, you will have to resort to the method known as dead reckoning, or DR for short (the 'dead' is, in fact, a corruption of 'ded.', short for 'deduced').

This consists of keeping a record of the courses and distances travelled since your last position fix. For example, if you estimate that you are walking at 4km (2.5 miles)/hr, and you travel for one hour on a course of 045°, then turn right onto 090° for 30 minutes, then go left on 000° for an hour and a half, your DR notes would show:

Time	Course	Distance
10.30	045	4km/2.5 miles
11.30	090	2km/1 mile
12.00	000	6km/4 miles
13.30		

Poor visibility

When trying to keep to a compass course in mist or heavy weather, one member of the party goes ahead to the limit of visibility (A), and then moves sideways until his waiting companion (B) is on an exact back bearing of the desired course. The companion then moves forward and the process is repeated.

You can then plot your DR position at 13.30 hours by plotting the consecutive courses and distances on the map from your last known position at 10.30 hours. If you are also able to fix your position at 13.30 hours, the difference between the DR position and the fix will reflect any errors that have affected the accuracy of your course and distance measurements.

For example, coping with a strong side wind when crossing an ice field, or having to cross a series of angled ridges on an arid plain might cause you to drift systematically to one side of your compass course. The difference between the DR position and the fix will show how much of an error these effects have caused, and allow you to take them into consideration in future DR navigation.

PRACTICE

As with all skills, practice makes perfect. You do not have to wait until you are out in the wilds to begin learning the practical side of navigation. There will be many occasions for you to be able to improve your map-reading and navigational skills. Here are a few suggestions:

● Take along a road map on any car or bus journey, and follow your route on the map, trying as much as possible to be aware of your position on the map at every stage of the journey.
● Better still, pretend you are the navigator of a rally car, whose job it is to tell the driver what to expect – use the map to predict which village, town or road junction will appear next, and which way to turn at each junction.
● Practise walking a compass course in the park. Lay down a small object on the grass – a coin will do, but do make it one you can afford to lose – then use your compass to follow any bearing for 100 paces. Then, turn around and follow the equivalent back bearing for the same distance, and see how close you are to the object.
● You can increase the difficulty of the previous exercise by walking three sides of a triangle (add or subtract 120° from the original bearing at each corner), or four sides of a square (add or subtract 90° at each corner).

NAVIGATING AT SEA

The methods described above can also be applied to navigation at sea, or when travelling by canoe on lakes and rivers. However, some extra knowledge is required for safe navigation in tidal waters.

The biggest difference between navigating on land and navigating at sea is that the sea is not a fixed and permanent surface – it moves, both up and down (with the tide) and from side to side (with tidal streams and currents). In addition, a boat may not be moving through the water in exactly the direction its bow is heading. If a wind is blowing strongly from one side, then any small boat, whether sailing yacht or kayak, will be pushed sideways to a certain degree. Because of these uncertainties, it is important to fix your position as often as possible at sea.

This section serves only as an introduction to navigating at sea. Anyone who plans to pilot a boat in tidal waters should consider undertaking a course of instruction in marine navigation.

UNDERSTANDING TIDES

One of the fundamental differences between navigating on land and at sea, is that the sea does not remain still. The level of the sea rises and falls twice a day as the earth's oceans respond to the gravitational pull of the moon. As the sea level changes, currents – known as tidal streams – flow back and forth; this effect is most visible in river mouths and in narrow channels.

The earth rotates once every 24 hours; however, the moon is also moving around the earth in the same direction. As a result, at any given meridian on the earth's surface, the moon passes directly overhead once every 24 hours and 50 minutes.

The moon's gravity creates two bulges in the surface of the earth's oceans - one directly beneath the moon, and another one on the far side of the planet. As the earth rotates, these two bulges are dragged around the planet, causing the sea level at any one place to rise and fall twice every 24 hours and 50 minutes.

TIDAL RANGE

This rise and fall is what we call the tide. The maximum and minimum height of the water level are called high tide and low tide respectively, although sailors usually refer to high water and low water. The difference in height between low and high tide is called the tidal range. In some places – for example, the eastern Mediterranean – the tidal range is very small, 1m (3ft) or less. In others – notably Brittany in France, the Channel Islands in the UK, and the eastern seaboard of Canada – the tidal range can be in excess of 14m (45ft).

At any given place, there is a usually a high tide once every 12 hours and 25 minutes; the time between high tide and the following low tide is roughly 6 hours 12 minutes. These are called semi-diurnal tides, and they occur throughout the middle latitudes.

Diurnal tides – with only one high water and one low water per day – occur mainly in the tropics, where the tidal range is very small. On the west coast of the USA and Canada, there is mixed tidal pattern, with two high and two low tides each day, but of different heights.

SPRING TIDES AND NEAP TIDES

The moon is not the only body whose gravitational attraction has an effect on the tides. The sun also exerts a pull on the earth's oceans, but its effect on the tide is weaker. The result is a regular, monthly variation in the heights of high and low water, called spring and neap tides.

A spring tide has nothing to do with the season of springtime, but means a tide with a larger than average range between high and low water. The opposite is a neap tide, with a smaller than average range between high and low water. In other words, high water is higher and low water is lower during a spring tide; and high water is lower and low water is higher during a neap tide.

Spring and neap tides follow the phases of the moon (see Chapter Four). Spring tides occur roughly every two weeks, a day or so after the full and new moon. Neap tides occur halfway between springs, a day or so after the moon's first and last quarter.

TIDE TABLES

If you are planning to go sailing, power-boating or kayaking in tidal waters, you will need to know the times and heights of the

Tidal information on the Internet

The following websites provide tidal predictions for most parts of the world:

Australia: www.ntf.flinders.edu.au/text/tides/tides.html

Canada: www.charts.gc.ca/chs/en/waterlevels

France: www.shom.fr/fr_page/fr_serv_prediction/ann_marees.htm

Germany: www.bsh.de/aktdat/wvd/wahome_ex.htm

New Zealand: www.hydro.linz.govt.nz/tides

UK & Ireland: www.hydro.gov.uk/tideprediction.cfm

USA: www.tidesonline.nos.noaa.gov

local tides. Tide tables covering whole countries and continents are published in the nautical almanacs carried by all commercial vessels and many pleasure yachts. However, these books are usually too large and expensive to be carried by small-boat sailors and canoeists.

A small booklet of annual tide tables is published for almost every popular sailing area – you can buy these cheaply from local sailing clubs, yacht chandlers, fishing tackle shops and tourist information offices. You can also find tidal information on the Internet.

Tide tables give the times and heights of high and low water for a particular place, usually a major port or harbour. The tidal height is usually quoted in metres, and is the height of the tide above chart datum (see Chapter One).

TIDAL HEIGHT

On every nautical chart, the depths of water printed on the chart are measured below an imaginary level called 'chart datum' (see Chapter One). This level is usually the lowest level to which the tide will ever fall, so at most times the actual depth of water will be greater than the depths shown on the chart.

If you study the areas of a chart close to the coast, you will see that they are shown coloured, and instead of showing the depths of water, the figures are underlined and represent what are called 'drying heights' – the height of the sea bed above chart datum. These 'drying' areas are the parts of the sea bed that are covered and uncovered by the rise and fall of the tide.

As these areas are often the ones that are used most by small-boat sailors and sea-kayakers, any navigator travelling in tidal, coastal waters needs to know how to calculate what the actual depth of water will be at any given time. To do this you will need to be able to calculate the tidal height at any given time.

CALCULATING TIDAL HEIGHTS

Tide tables list the times and tidal heights – the heights of water above chart datum – for every high water and low water at a particular place in a particular year. These are usually listed in the following form:

March
5   03.22   1.2
Su   09.18   5.1
       15.37   1.3
       21.33   5.0

In this example, on Sunday, 5 March, high water (HW) occurs at 09.18 hours with a tidal height of 5.1m (16.7ft), and at 21.33 hours with a height of 5m (16.2ft). Low water (LW) occurs at 03.22 hours and 15.37 hours with heights of 1.2m (3.9ft) and 1.3m (4.2ft) respectively.

To calculate the tidal height at any time between high and low water, you need to interpolate between the listed heights. The most accurate way to do this is by using a graph called a tidal curve, which you can find in nautical almanacs and most tide tables; there is a different curve for each location.

In areas with normal semi-diurnal tides, you can make an approximate calculation using the 'rule of twelfths'. This assumes that there are roughly six hours between low and high water, and that the tide will rise or fall by one-twelfth of the total range in the first hour; by two-twelfths in the second hour; by three-twelfths in the third hour, and again in the fourth hour; by two-twelfths in the fifth hour; and by one-twelfth in the sixth hour.

Using this rule and the table above, we can calculate the approximate height of tide at 11.30 hours on Sunday, 5 March. The tidal range at this time will be the difference between the HW and LW heights on either side, ie

Tidal range = 5.1 - 1.3 = 3.8m

As 11.30 hours is approximately two hours after HW at 9.18am, the rule of twelfths says that the tide will have fallen by $\frac{1}{12} + \frac{2}{12} = \frac{3}{12}$ (or $\frac{1}{4}$) of the total range:

Fall of tide = $\frac{1}{4}$ x 3.8 = 0.95m (3ft)

We then subtract the fall of tide from the previous HW height to give the tidal height at 11.30 hours:

Tidal height = 5.1 - 0.95 = 4.15m (14ft)

To find the actual depth of water at any given place on the chart at 11.30 hours, we add any depths below chart datum to the tidal height, or subtract any drying heights above chart datum from the tidal height. So a channel shown on the chart as having a depth of 2m (6ft) would actually have just over 6m (18ft) of water, while a sandbank shown with a drying height of 2m (6ft) would have just over 2m (6ft) of water.

PLOTTING A COURSE TO MAKE ALLOWANCE FOR A TIDAL STREAM

Because the entire body of water on which a boat is floating may be moving in response to the tide, the compass course that a boat steers through the water may not be the same as its course over the ground. (You can visualize a boat's course over the ground by imagining its shadow moving over the seabed.)

Anyone who has seen a ferry boat crossing a river with a strong current will recognize this effect. In order to counter the current, the ferry master points the vessel's bow slightly upstream. So the boat's heading, or the course steered through the water, differs from the course made good over the ground (a straight line across the river). In tidal waters, this effect must be taken into account when you are calculating a compass course towards your destination.

Imagine that you are in a sea kayak, and you want to paddle across a channel to a bay on an island that is 1.852km (1 nautical mile) away. You know from the chart that the bay lies directly north (000°). The chart also tells you that the tidal stream will be flowing east at 1 knot. If you set off heading 000°, then the tide will sweep you to the east of your desired destination. If the bay is visible, and you continually alter course to keep pointing towards it, you will still be swept off course and finish by paddling almost directly upstream to your destination. So what course should you steer to take the most direct line towards your objective? Study the illustration opposite.

● Begin by plotting the course you want on the chart – this is the course over the ground that you want to follow (in this example, 000°). **AB**
● Next, draw a second line to represent the tidal stream. This line is a vector, which means that it has magnitude as well as direction – that is, its length is proportional to the velocity of the tidal stream. To keep it simple, make 1cm (0.4in) represent 1 knot. **AC**
● In this example, your paddling speed through the water is going to be two knots. From the downstream end of the tidal vector, use compasses or a ruler to find the point where a vector line 2cm (0.8in) long (representing 2 knots) intersects the line of your desired course. **B**
● The direction of this vector is the course to steer. In the example, it is 334° true. Convert this to magnetic by correcting for declination before use. **CB**
● The length of the line between A and B tells you the speed you will make good over the ground. In this case it is 1.7cm (0.7in), which represents 1.7 knots, so it will take you about 35 minutes to make the crossing.

The actual lengths of lines AC and CB are not important, as long as both are proportional to the speeds they represent.

Vectors

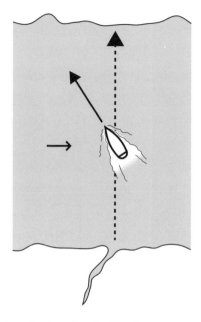

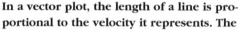

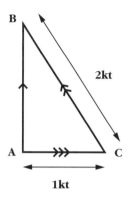

In a vector plot, the length of a line is proportional to the velocity it represents. The tide (AC) is 1 knot; the boat's speed through the water (CB) is 2 knots; and the boat's speed over the ground (AB) is 1.7 knots.

FIXING YOUR POSITION AT SEA

Because a boat at sea is subject to the vagaries of wind and tide, remembering to fix your position frequently is more important than on land, where you can stop and consult your map more easily. It is impossible to stop altogether at sea unless you drop an anchor. In addition, the effects of wind and tide are continuously introducing errors into your calculations of course and speed.

RESECTION

Resection using three bearings (see the section earlier in this chapter) is the traditional way of obtaining an accurate position fix at sea. This is because taking an accurate bearing of a landmark on a boat moving around on the waves is more difficult than doing so on dry land. As a result, errors are more common, and you will almost always get a 'cocked hat'. Choose landmarks that are as close as possible, as this will reduce the potential error.

THE RUNNING FIX

When travelling along a coast, you can get a 'running fix' by taking two consecutive bearings of a single landmark, provided you know how far you have travelled between taking the bearings. Having measured the bearings and the times that you took them, there are two methods of plotting a running fix. The first is used where there is no tidal drift.

For example, you take a bearing of a lighthouse at time t1 (see the illustration on page 62) when it lies at an angle of 45° to your heading – in this case, your heading is 090°

The running fix

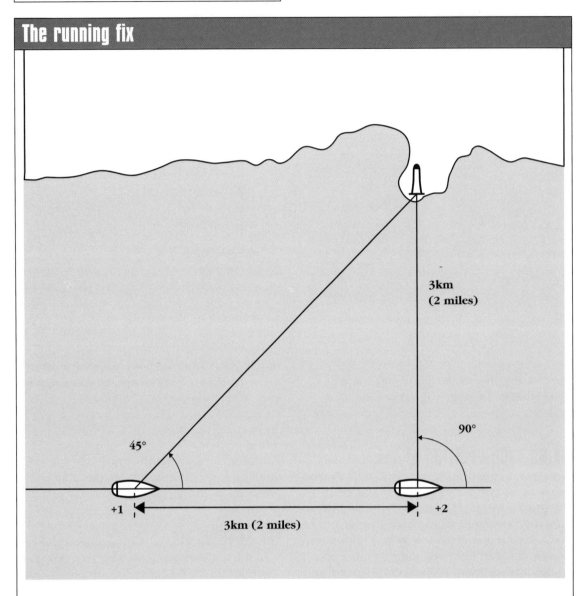

The standard running fix is based on the geometry of a right-angled isosceles triangle (that is, one in which two sides are of equal length). If your boat is moving along a straight course, and you note the times t1 and t2 at which a landmark bears 45° off the bow and 90° off the bow respectively, then the distance you have travelled between t1 and t2 is equal to the distance between you and the landmark at t2. For example, imagine you are sailing at 4 knots on a compass course of 090°, and you note that the lighthouse bears 045° (i.e. 45° off your bow) at 10.30am, and then 000° (90° off your bow) at 11.00am. The distance you have covered between the two bearings is 3km (2 miles), so your position at 11.00am is 3km (2 miles) due south of the lighthouse.

and the lighthouse bears 045°. If you then wait until time t2, when the lighthouse lies at an angle of 90° to your heading (ie when it bears 000°), then the distance (d) you have travelled between t1 and t2 is equal to your distance from the lighthouse at time t2. This is equivalent to finding two intersecting position lines – the bearing 000°, and the circular position line at distance (d) from the lighthouse. You can then plot your position on the chart.

The second method is used when there is tidal drift. First you plot the lines of both bearings from the lighthouse on the chart. Then, from any point on the first line, you plot a vector representing the course and distance steered between time t1 and t2. From the end of this line, you then plot a tidal vector representing the distance and direction the tide will have set you off course between t1 and t2. Finally, from the end of the tidal vector, you draw a line parallel to the first bearing; where this intersects the second bearing is your position at time t2.

The running fix method is also known as doubling the angle on the bow – it will work with any two pairs of bearings, provided that the second makes twice as big an angle with your heading as the second, (eg 30° and 60°). It is also important, of course, that you maintain a constant heading between t1 and t2.

The accuracy of a running fix depends on the accuracy of the bearings, and the accuracy of the boat's direction and distance travelled over the ground.

NAVIGATION MARKS

Coastal areas contain many artificial navigation marks – such as buoys and lighthouses – which have been installed mainly for the benefit of large commercial vessels. As they are shown on nautical charts, they are also of use to small-boat sailors, not only to indicate hazards but as landmarks from which to take bearings when fixing your position.

BUOYS

Buoys (pronounced 'boys' in the UK, and 'boo-eys' in the USA) are floating markers that are moored over or close to navigational hazards, or along the edges of safe channels. Their positions are usually shown on nautical charts.

Buoys are distinguished by their shape, colour and topmark (a bold shape attached to the top of the buoy), and by flashing lights. There are two international systems of buoyage, both of which are in widespread use around the world.

Lateral buoys

Lateral buoys are used to mark the edges of channels and the entrances to harbours and river mouths. There are two varieties of lateral buoy – port-hand and starboard hand. To avoid shallow water or other hazards indicated by lateral marks, you leave port-hand buoys to port (left) and starboard-hand buoys to starboard (right), when travelling with the direction of buoyage. Going the other way, against the direction of buoyage, these rules are obviously reversed.

The direction of buoyage is always into a harbour, upstream on a river, and in the direction of the flood tide elsewhere. In areas where the direction of buoyage is not obvious, it is marked on the chart with a large arrow ('C' on diagram on page 64).

Port-hand buoys (A) are coloured red, are can-shaped or have can-shaped topmarks, and if lit have a flashing red light. Starboard-hand buoys (B) are coloured green, are conical or have conical topmarks, and if lit have a flashing green light.

Cardinal buoys

Cardinal buoys are used to mark various kinds of hazard. There are four kinds – north, south, east and west – distinguished by the orientation of their two conical topmarks, and the pattern of yellow and black paint on their bodies.

North cardinal buoys are moored to the north of the hazard, east cardinal buoys to the east, and so on. So, to keep clear of any hazard, you should pass to the north of a north buoy, to the east of an east buoy, and so on.

Mark Topmark Body
North buoy (D) up/up black/yellow
East buoy (E) up/down black/yellow/black
South buoy (F) down/down yellow/black
West buoy (G) down/up yellow/black/yellow

You can easily remember how to recognize north and south marks by imagining that the conical topmarks are pointing up (north) or down (south) on a compass dial. To tell east and west apart, remember that the topmark on a west buoy (W) looks like a (W)ine glass.

Other buoys

Other kinds of buoys include:
● Safe water marks (H) - spar or spherical buoy with vertical red and white stripes - marks safe water in the middle of a shipping channel
● Isolated danger marks (I) - spar or pillar with horizontal red and black stripes - marks small, isolated danger with navigable water all around
● Special mark (J) - any kind of buoy or mark coloured yellow all over - marks various features such as the end of sewage outfall pipes, traffic separation lanes, or offshore dumping grounds.

LIGHTHOUSES

A lighthouse is a prominent structure - usually a tower - built on headlands, islands and isolated rocks along the coast. They contain powerful lights that warn mariners of danger, and allow navigators to fix their position by taking bearings of them.

By day, lighthouses can only be distinguished by their appearance. For this reason,

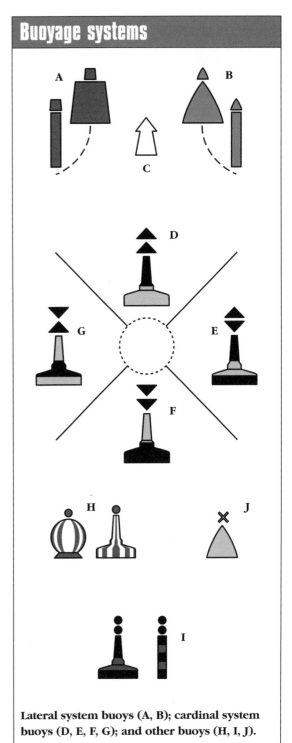

Buoyage systems

Lateral system buoys (A, B); cardinal system buoys (D, E, F, G); and other buoys (H, I, J).

lighthouses in a particular area are often painted with different patterns (eg plain white, plain red, red and white stripes) so that they can be told apart. At night, they can be recognized by the character of the light they show. Character refers to the pattern of light and darkness that a light displays.

A light can be of four types – fixed, flashing, occulting and isophase.

● A fixed light is simply a steady, unchanging light
● A flashing light is mostly dark, but displays a set pattern of flashes. Flashes can be single, or in groups of two, three or more
● An occulting light is mostly on, but displays a set pattern of dark phases
● An isophase light shows equal periods of light and dark

The character of a light is described in abbreviated form on the chart, beside its symbol. The period of a light is the time (in seconds) it takes to repeat its pattern. Here are some examples, using the abbreviations used on British charts:

● Fl. 5s (a flashing light, with one flash every five seconds)
● Fl. (3) 15s (a flashing light, with three flashes every 15 seconds)
● Occ. (2) 10s (an occulting light, with two dark phases every 10 seconds)
● Iso. 10s (an isophase light, showing five seconds of light and five seconds of darkness every 10 seconds)

The information on the chart will also tell you the height above sea level of the light in metres, and its visible range in nautical miles. The standard abbreviations for light characteristics are explained in the chart legend.

CHAPTER FOUR

Navigating with Nature

In an emergency you may find yourself forced to navigate without the aid of map and compass. Fortunately, the natural world provides plenty of clues for the wilderness navigator. But first, you need to learn how to read them.

All good navigators, even when using map and compass or GPS, are continually picking up clues about direction from their environment, noting the position of the sun, the length and direction of shadows, the run of river valleys and mountain ridges, the direction of wind and swell at sea.

Picking up clues is a good habit to cultivate. Not only does it make you more aware of the environment around you, it also builds up a general awareness of which nat-

ural indicators are reliable, as you have the luxury of being able to check them using proper equipment.

Being aware of naturally occurring aids to navigation is important, as they can often be the first indication that you have wandered off course. If you emerge from a section of thick forest with the sun straight ahead of you – when it had been to your left when you entered the trees – it is wise to stop and check your map and compass. Just as importantly, natural direction indicators can save your life if you have to navigate in an emergency without map and compass.

Most of the techniques described in this chapter do not provide you with a permanent record of direction, so once you have determined direction from a sunrise bearing, or found out which way is north using a shadow-stick, you will have to relate that knowledge to the landmarks around you.

The best way to do this is to draw a sketch map, noting all the visible landmarks and features around you, related to a north point determined by your observation of some natural direction indicator. Keep adding to your map as you move, checking your direction and position as often as possible, and keep careful notes of the distance and direction in which you have travelled.

The real secret of navigating with nature is to practise whenever you can, with a map and compass for backup. Develop the habit of keeping one eye on the sun or the stars, and be on the lookout for any natural signs that might help you find your way. Do not wait for an emergency before you start learning to navigate with nature.

READING NATURE'S SIGNS

Part of every experienced navigator's routine is to cultivate an awareness of things in their environment that indicate direction. These indicators may be permanent, like the general run of mountain ridges; or they may be temporary, like the sculpting of snow by a westerly gale, or the build-up of ice crystals on the upwind faces of rocks.

If you are planning a trip to an area that you have never visited before, then you should find out as much as possible about any natural direction indicators that might be of use. The most basic, and most useful, is learning what could be termed the 'grain' of the country. In which direction do the main rivers flow? In which direction does the coastline run? In which direction are

the main mountain ridges aligned? And most importantly in an emergency, in which direction will the nearest help be found?

LANDSCAPE INDICATORS

In some parts of the world the landscape has a distinctive 'grain' – the main mountain ridges and valleys run fairly straight and parallel. For example, in the Appalachian mountains of Virginia and West Virginia in the USA, the ridges and valleys run predominantly from southwest to northeast, and on the Adriatic coast of Croatia the mainland ridges and valleys and the long, thin offshore islands all run northwest–southeast. In this type of terrain, if you are following a major valley, then you have a good idea in which direction you are travelling.

In desert environments, sand dunes are usually aligned with the prevailing winds; provided you know the direction of the prevailing wind, the dunes can be a useful direction indicator. There are different kinds of sand dunes, however, which have different relationships to the wind. Classic transverse dunes, which occur in areas with a large amount of sand, are oriented perpendicular to the wind, with a gentle upwind slope and a steep downwind slope. However, in some areas with a limited sand supply – notably the vast Sand Ridge Desert of central Australia – long, thin longitudinal dunes develop, which are aligned parallel to the prevailing wind.

PLANT AND ANIMAL INDICATORS

One traditional clue to direction that is often recommended in the Northern hemisphere is that moss and lichen grow more thickly on the north side of an isolated tree trunk. In reality, the growth of moss and lichen is influenced by many factors, and this can be an unreliable indicator. Only use it in combination with other direction indicators.

More useful indicators are trees and bushes that have been bent over and deformed by

Reading nature's signs

Looking for moss and lichen on the north side of a tree trunk (in the Northern hemisphere) is not a reliable indicator of direction. Use this method with care.

the prevailing winds — provided, of course, that you know which direction the prevailing winds blow from. On many exposed westerly coasts in Britain and Ireland, you can see trees whose branches all grow almost parallel to the ground, bent to shape by the strong southwesterly winds.

In mountainous areas, it is often possible to tell north-facing slopes from south-facing ones by the amount and type of vegetation growing on them. Southerly slopes (facing the sun) often have thicker and taller growth. Another pointer is to look for snow patches that last into spring – in northern latitudes, these are usually on the northern and northeastern slopes of the mountains.

In certain parts of the world there are specific plants that can provide clues as to direction. In North America, there is the compass plant, or pilotweed (*Silphium laciniatum*), which aligns its leaves in a north–south direction. The compass barrel cactus (*Ferocactus cylindraeus*), native to the southwest USA and northern Mexico, grows faster on its shady side and ends up slanted towards the south.

At sea, flocks of sea birds flying overhead at dusk are almost certain to be heading for a roosting place on land (though this may only be offshore islands and not necessarily the mainland).

In northern Australia, termite mounds can be up to 4m (12ft) tall, 2.5m (7.5ft) wide and 1m (3ft) thick, and are always oriented with their long axis running north–south.

USING THE SUN TO FIND DIRECTION

Plant and animal indicators can be useful, but by far the best place to look for a natural compass is the sky. The relationship of the earth to the sun is the easiest and most reliable indicator of direction that you can use.

In order to use the sun to measure time and direction with any accuracy, you need to know the basics of how the solar system works. The earth rotates once every 24 hours, and as it does so the sun appears to move across the sky. Looking down from above the north pole, the earth rotates anticlockwise, from west to east. As a consequence, the sun appears to move across the sky from east to west, rising in the east and setting in the west.

If you are in the Northern hemisphere, then the sun will be due south when it reaches its highest point in the sky. In the Southern hemisphere, it will be due north at this point. Close to the equator, it will be almost directly overhead.

However, the sun does not always rise and set exactly due east and west at all times. There is a seasonal – and, fortunately, entirely predictable – variation. Because of the tilt in the earth's axis, the point on the eastern horizon where the sun rises each day creeps slowly north and south with the seasons.

In the Northern hemisphere at the winter solstice (the shortest day of the year, around 21 December), the sunrise is at its farthest south. Over the following months the sunrise creeps slowly north and the days lengthen. At the spring equinox (around 21 March), the sun rises exactly due east everywhere in the world. The sunrise bearing continues to move north until it reaches a maximum at the summer solstice (the longest day of the year, around 21 June), then starts to creep south again. At the autumn equinox (around 21 September), the sunrise is exactly due east again, and it keeps moving south until the winter solstice when the whole cycle begins again.

The sunset displays exactly the same variations, with the sun setting south of west in winter, north of west in summer, and exactly due west at the equinoxes. These variations are more extreme at higher latitudes, but much less noticeable close to the equator.

In the Southern hemisphere, the winter solstice is on 21 June. At this point the sunrise is at its furthest north. Over the following months the sunrise creeps slowly south and the days lengthen. At the spring equinox (around 21 September), the sun rises exactly due east. The sunrise bearing continues to move south until it reaches a maximum at the summer solstice (around 21 December), then starts to creep north again. At the autumn equinox (around 21 March), the sunrise is exactly due east again, and it keeps moving north until the winter solstice.

Using simple tables, it is easy to predict the exact bearing of sunrise and sunset for any place on earth, provided you know the approximate latitude and time of year (see boxed text, Sunrise and sunset bearings).

Taking a sunrise or sunset bearing is the most accurate direction line that can easily be obtained without any navigational tools whatever, provided you have the chart and table shown on page 72. Of course, you can always memorize the details of the chart and the maximum amplitude – the amount by which the sunrise or sunset deviates from due east or due west – for the area you are travelling in. If it helps, draw a chart or even scratch one on the ground to make your calculation.

You can record the direction of sunrise or sunset by

Sunrise and sunset bearings

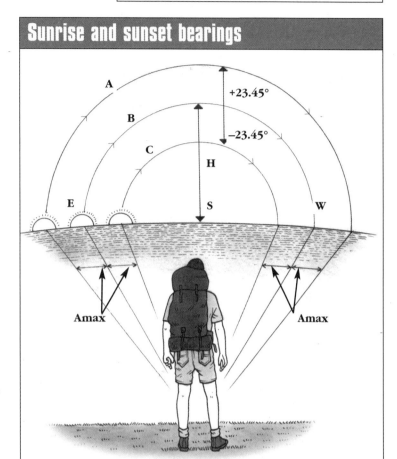

The course of the sun through the sky varies with the time of year. The diagram shows the relative positions of the sun (seen from the Northern hemisphere) at the summer solstice (A), the equinoxes (B) and the winter solstice (C). The angular height of the sun above the horizon at noon during the equinoxes (H) is equal to 90° – your latitude. This value increases in summer to a maximum of H + 23.45° at the

summer solstice, and decreases in winter to a minimum of H – 23.45° at the winter solstice.

At the equinoxes, the sun rises exactly due east (E) and sets exactly due west (W). The bearings of sunrise and sunset move north in summer and south in winter by an amount known as the amplitude, which reaches a maximum (Amax) at the solstices. The value of Amax varies with latitude (see the amplitude chart on page 72).

Sunrise/sunset bearing calculator

Amplitude table

Latitude (N or S)	Max. Amplitude
5	24°
10	24°
15	24°
20	25°
25	26°
30	27°
35	29°
40	31°
45	34°
50	38°
55	44°
60	53°

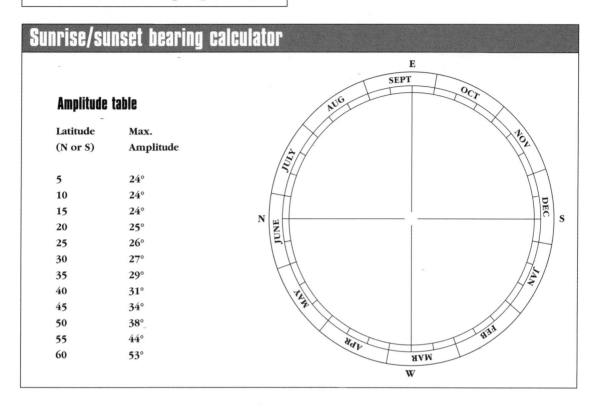

using a fixed rock or stick as a foresight, and a second movable rock or stick as a back-sight. You can then find north or south, or measure bearings from this direction line by eye, or more accurately by using a makeshift protractor.

A piece of string, divided into 12 equal units marked with ink or knots, can be used to measure angles. Arrange it into a triangle of four units on each side (peg out the corners with sticks), and all the angles will be 60°. Arrange it into a triangle with sides of three, four and five units, and the three angles will be 90°, 60° and 30°.

To find out the bearings of sunrise and sunset for your location on a given day:
● Using the amplitude table, find out the maximum amplitude (Amax) for your latitude, interpolating if necessary.
●Transfer this value to the horizontal baseline on the chart so that the centre point is zero and either end of the baseline equals Amax.
● Find today's date on the circumference of the chart and drop or raise a line from it perpendicular to the horizontal axis and read off the amplitude (A) for that day.
● Apply the appropriate calculation in the table below.

Bearing calculation

For north amplitudes:
Sunrise bearing = 90° - A
Sunset bearing = 270° + A

For south amplitudes:
Sunrise bearing = 90° + A
Sunset bearing = 270° - A

Edinburgh example

Here is the calculation for Edinburgh, Scotland (latitude 56° N) on 5 November:

● Edinburgh's latitude, 56° N is ⅕ of the way between 55 and 60, so using interpolation its Amax is around ⅕ of the way between 44° and 53° – about 46°.

● Scaling the baseline appropriately will give you the chart below (which will apply to everywhere in the world with latitude 56° N or 56° S).

● Dropping a line perpendicular to the horizontal axis from the point corresponding to 5 November on the circumference of the chart gives a south amplitude of 32°.

● The sunrise bearing for Edinburgh on 5 November will therefore be 90° + 32° = 122°, and the sunset bearing will be 270° - 32° = 238°.

USING SHADOWS TO FIND DIRECTION

As the sun moves across the sky from east to west, the shadows it casts move across the ground in the opposite direction, from west to east (this is true in both northern and southern hemispheres). You can demonstrate this simple fact by creating a direction line on the ground. Use a straight stick at least 1m (3ft) in length – a trekking pole or ski pole is ideal, but a fence post, branch of a tree or large piece of driftwood will do. The longer the stick, the more accurate the direction line.

Method one (approximate)

● Find a level and fairly smooth area of ground and place the stick vertically in the ground so that it casts a clear shadow. Mark

Using a shadow stick

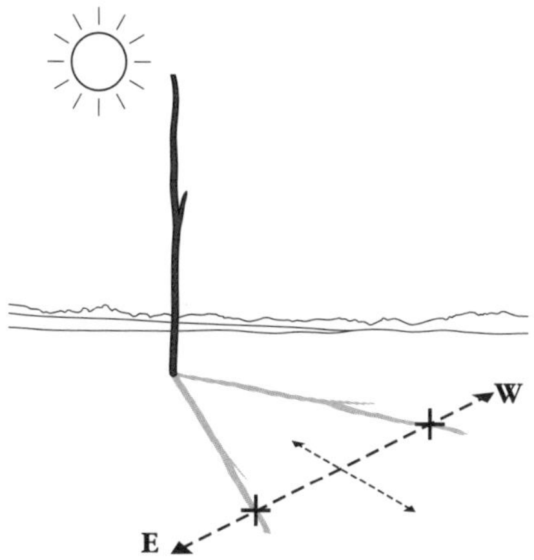

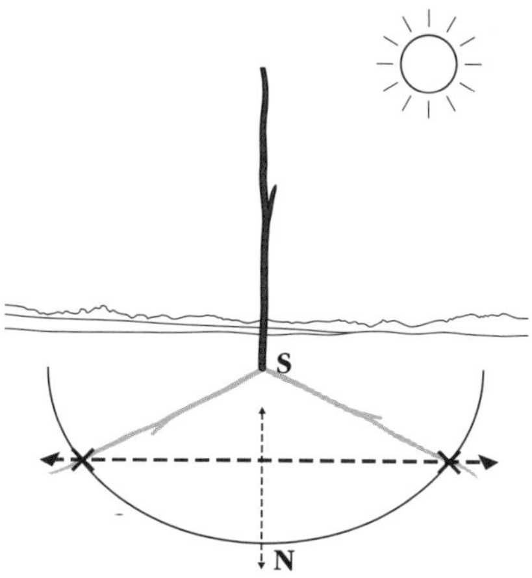

You can use the movement of the shadow cast by a stick to find direction. A line joining the tips of two consecutive shadows runs approximately E–W. The second method, which requires a wait of several hours, is the more accurate.

the tip of the shadow with a pebble, twig or other marker. This first mark will always be the western one, whether you are in the northern or the southern hemisphere.

● Wait for at least 15 minutes, until the shadow has moved a few centimetres, or an inch or more - the longer you wait, the more accurate your direction line will be - and place a second marker on the new tip of the shadow.

● Mark out a straight line joining the two markers - use another stick or pole, or a piece of string stretched tight. This line will be oriented approximately east–west.

● If you now stand with your shoulders parallel to this line, with the first shadow-marker on your left and the second on your right, you will be facing due north.

The second method is more accurate but involves waiting around for a few hours, so is only suitable if you have the time to spare - perhaps during desert travel while resting up during the hottest part of the day.

Method 2 (more accurate)

● Set up your stick or pole as for method one, and make the first shadow mark around mid-morning.

● Stretch a piece of string between the base of the stick and the mark, and use it to scratch a semicircle on the ground from the first shadow mark - clockwise in the Northern hemisphere, anticlockwise in the Southern hemisphere.

● You will now have to wait for a few hours. As the sun climbs towards noon, the stick shadow will shift to the east and shorten, moving away from the arc you have drawn on the ground. Then, as the sun begins to go down, the shadow will lengthen again, and around mid-afternoon the tip of the shadow will again touch the arc - you should mark this point.

● Join the two markers to obtain an accurate east–west line. Orient yourself to the markers as in method one to find north.

USING A WATCH TO FIND DIRECTION

If you have an analog watch (one with hands), you can use it to find an approximate direction from the sun. For this technique to work, the watch must be using true local time (that is, without any change made for daylight-saving time). The further away from the equator you are, the more accurate this method will be. In middle latitudes it can produce an error of up to 20 degrees.

Hold the watch face horizontally, and (in the Northern hemisphere) point the hour hand towards the sun. You can do this more accurately by aligning the hour hand with the shadow from a vertical object - the corner of a building, a fence post or a weighted string will do.

Bisect the angle between the hour hand and the 12 o'clock mark on the watch face - this direction is south. For example, if your watch is showing exactly 4.00 pm with the hour hand pointing at the sun, then the 2 o'clock mark on the watch face (halfway between 4 and 12) will be pointing due south.

Note - before 06.00 and after 18.00 hours, this method will indicate north rather than south, but at these times you would do better to get an accurate sunrise or sunset bearing.

In the Southern hemisphere, the technique is slightly different: point the 12 o'clock mark on the watch face at the sun, and then bisect the angle between it and the hour hand - this direction is north (or south before 06.00 and after 18.00 hours).

And if you only have a digital watch? No problem - just draw a clock face on a piece of paper, or scratch one on the ground, draw in a 12 o'clock mark and the hour hand showing the correct time, and orient it as already described.

If your watch is set to daylight-saving time, either turn it back an hour, or bisect the angle between the hour hand and the 1 o'clock mark.

Using an analog watch

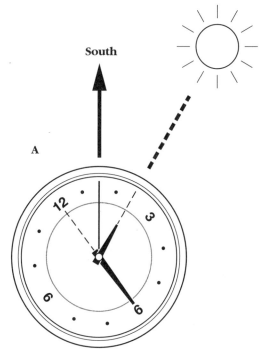

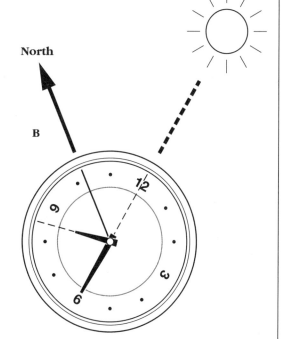

An analog watch can be used to gain a rough idea of direction from the sun. In the Northern hemisphere (A), point the hour hand at the sun and bisect the angle between it and the 12 o' clock mark to find south. In the Southern hemisphere (B), point the 12 o' clock mark at the sun and bisect the angle between it and the hour hand to find north.

FINDING TIME AND DIRECTION FROM THE MOON

The moon orbits the earth once every 29½ days, but during the course of one night you will see it traverse the sky along roughly the same path followed by the sun, rising in the east and setting in the west. However, its appearance – full, new, half or crescent – and the time that it rises and sets, will depend on what point it is at in its cycle (it rises and sets around 50 minutes later each night). The so-called phases of the moon depend simply on the angle between it and a straight line drawn between the earth and the sun.

The moon is described as a new moon when it is between the earth and the sun. Its dark side is then turned towards us, and we can see it only dimly and briefly in the west around the time of sunset. At the time of the new moon, the moon rises and sets at the same time as the sun, and the nights are moonless.

About two weeks after the new moon, the moon is on the opposite side of the earth to the sun, so that its bright side is turned

Solstices and equinoxes

The earth's axis of rotation is tilted at an angle of 23½°. As the earth orbits the sun in the course of a year, it is this tilt that accounts for the difference in the amount of daylight between winter and summer. The Northern hemisphere experiences winter when the north pole is tilted away from the sun, and summer when it is tilted towards the sun.

In the Northern hemisphere, the point in the earth's orbit when the north pole is tilted away from the sun is called the winter solstice (21 December). The point diametrically opposite the winter solstice, where the north pole is tilted away from the sun, is called the summer solstice (21 June). In the Southern hemisphere the seasons are reversed, so the southern winter solstice occurs on 21 June and the southern summer solstice on 21 December.

The word solstice comes from the Latin, meaning 'sun stands still', because at these times the point on the horizon where the sun rises appears to stop and change direction.

The two points in the earth's orbit halfway between the solstices, where the tilt of the earth's axis lies side-on to the sun, are called the vernal equinox (or spring equinox) and the autumnal equinox. The word equinox comes from the Latin, meaning 'equal night', because at these times every place on earth experiences exactly 12 hours of darkness and 12 hours of daylight.

---

towards us. This is the full moon, which rises in the east as the sun is setting in the west, and it shines all night long – on a clear night with a full moon, the moonlight is often strong enough to cast a shadow, and you can use the approximate shadow-stick method described above to find direction.

During the period between new and full moon, the moon is said to be waxing. Each evening at sunset, the moon is a little higher in the sky, and a little more of it is illuminated. About a week after the new moon, the moon is at right angles to the line between earth and sun, so that at sunset we see it high in the sky with the west-facing half illuminated; this the first-quarter moon.

Between the full moon and new moon, the moon is said to be waning. A week after full moon comes the last-quarter moon, which does not rise until midnight, and is sitting high in the sky at dawn.

Between new and first-quarter, from last-quarter back to new, we see a crescent moon. Between first-quarter and full, and from full to last-quarter, the moon is described as gibbous.

You can tell roughly what time it is by the appearance of the moon as it rises in the east.
- Full moon – rises at 18.00 hours
- Waning gibbous moon – rises around 21.00 hours
- Last-quarter moon (with the eastern half, the left-hand half in the northern hemisphere, illuminated) – rises at midnight
- Waning crescent moon – rises around 03.00 hours
- New moon – rises at 06.00 hours
- First-quarter moon (with the western half, the right-hand half in the Northern hemisphere, illuminated) – rises at noon, and can sometimes be seen in the eastern sky in the afternoon.

Seen from the Southern hemisphere, the last quarter moon has its right-hand half illuminated, and the first quarter moon has its left-hand half illuminated.

Major constellations

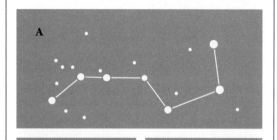

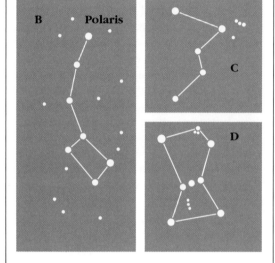

Famous constellations in the Northern hemisphere:

A – Ursa Major, the Plough,
  or the Big Dipper
B – Ursa Minor, or the Little Bear,
  with Polaris at the tip of its tail
C – Cassiopeia
D – Orion

FINDING DIRECTION FROM THE STARS

On a clear night in the wilds, far away from the light pollution of towns and cities, the starlit night sky is an awesome sight.

Night-time navigation is not for beginners. Quite apart from the difficulty of the navigation itself, you must consider the dangers of moving over rough country in darkness – there is always the possibility of stumbling off the trail or tripping on branches or boulders. A sprained ankle, or worse, should not be risked unless navigation is absolutely necessary.

However, the night sky does offer a wealth of useful direction indicators. You need only identify a few constellations in order to be able to navigate by the stars, and the chances are that you are already familiar with them.

NORTHERN HEMISPHERE

The most useful constellation in the northern sky is known in Britain as the Plough, and in North America as the Big Dipper (it is part of a larger constellation called Ursa Major, or the Great Bear). The two stars on the outer lip of the Plough, opposite the 'handle', are called Dubhe and Merak. Together they are known as 'the pointers' because they point to Polaris, the Pole Star.

Once you have identified the Plough, mentally extrapolate a line through the two pointer stars for about five times the distance between them, and they will lead you to Polaris. Polaris lies within a degree of the celestial north pole, and is an accurate and reliable indicator of geographic north.

The Plough is almost always visible in a clear night sky at latitudes higher than 50 degrees north. If it is obscured by hills or below the horizon, then you should still be able to see Cassiopeia, a distinctive W- or M-shaped constellation (depending which way up it is) that lies on the opposite side of Polaris from the Plough.

To find Polaris using Cassiopeia, imagine a straight line joining the tips of the two outside arms of the W (or M), then project a line at right angles to this one for about 4½ times the span of the W (or M). This should lead you to Polaris. It is easier to do than to describe (see the diagram on page 78).

Finding Polaris

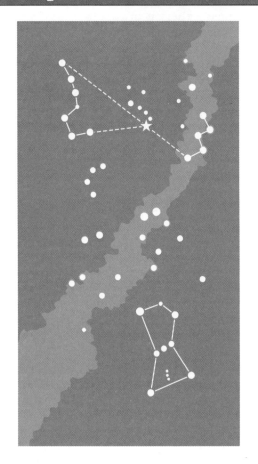

Cassiopeia and the Plough/Big Dipper lie on opposite sides of Polaris (the Pole Star).

Once you have located Polaris, and decided which direction you need to travel, you can hold a reasonably steady course by choosing a bright star that lies in your direction of travel and heading towards it. Remember, however, that the stars are rotating around Polaris at a rate of 15° per hour, so check your heading against the Pole Star every 20 minutes or so and choose another star if necessary.

SOUTHERN HEMISPHERE

The southern hemisphere also has a star neatly positioned at the celestial pole, but unfortunately it is so dim as to be invisible to the naked eye. Fortunately, there is a distinctive constellation that will help you to find south. The Southern Cross contains five stars in a cruciform pattern. The white stars on the Australian flag represent the Southern Cross.

Finding direction from the Southern Cross is a little trickier than using Polaris. Once you have found the Cross in the night sky, draw an imaginary line extending through the two main stars (see diagram opposite) – the south celestial pole lies along this line. To help you visualize the correct spot, use the two bright trailing stars located anticlockwise from the Southern Cross; draw a line between them, and extend a line at right angles from it – where this intersects with the first line is the location of the south celestial pole.

Once again, it is easier to do than to describe. However, if you find it too difficult to imagine, wait until the Southern Cross is standing vertically in the sky. At this point, south lies on the horizon directly beneath the Cross.

ORION

The constellation of Orion, recognized by its 'belt' of three closely spaced stars in a straight line, lies right on the celestial equator, and therefore rises almost exactly due east and sets almost exactly due west, no matter what your latitude is. It is prominent in the night sky in winter in the Northern hemisphere and in summer in the Southern hemisphere.

Orion is really only of use for finding west, which is indicated by the point where Orion's belt dips below the horizon as it sets. Unless you are a skilled stargazer, you will have no idea of where it is going to rise until most or all of the constellation is well above the horizon.

The Southern Cross

The most distinctive constellation in the Southern hemisphere is the Southern Cross, which is accompanied by two bright 'trailing' stars to its east (left). The Coalsack, a dark nebula, forms a starless area immediately southeast of the Southern Cross. When the Southern Cross appears upright in the night sky (ie with its long axis vertical), a line dropped vertically down to the horizon beneath it indicates geographic south.

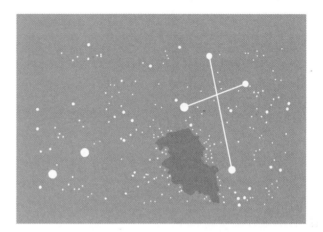

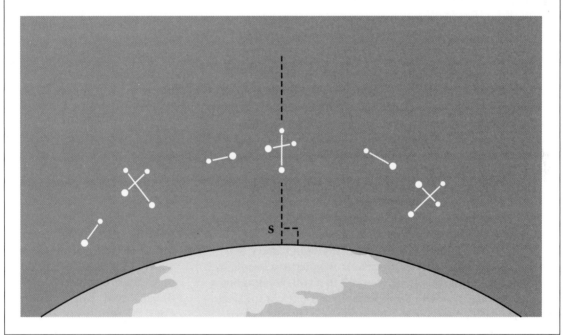

FINDING DIRECTION FROM ANY STAR

If your view of the sky is limited, perhaps by mountains or trees, you can still find an approximate direction by choosing any bright star (preferably one not too close to the poles). Note its position relative to a peak on the horizon, or by sighting along a stick pushed into the ground, or by propping a rifle against a rock or stick and using the gun sight.

Wait 15–20 minutes and then note in which direction the star has moved.

Magnetizing a makeshift compass needle

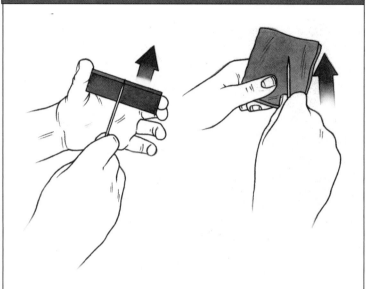

You can magnetize a needle by repeatedly stroking it with a magnet. A small magnet and a sewing needle should be part of every survival kit, but in an emergency you can find a magnet in the loudspeaker or headphones of a radio set. If you don't have a magnet, stroking with a piece of silk or nylon, or even a piece of stone, will do, but the effect will be much weaker and will need 'topping up' more often.

Stroke the needle in one direction only, and always in the same direction – mark one end of the needle, to be sure you always stroke it the same way. To remain useful, it will probably need to be topped up three or four times a day.

If you have a battery (an ordinary flashlight battery will do) and some wire, you can effectively magnetize a needle by wrapping the wire round and round it in a coil, and passing a current through the wire for at least five minutes. If the wire is not insulated, wrap the needle in paper or plastic before you wrap the wire around it.

The following rules are for the Northern hemisphere:
- Upward – it is in the east
- Downward – it is in the west
- Left – it is in the north
- Right – it is in the south.

In the southern hemisphere, the equivalent rules are:
- Upward – it is in the west
- Downward – it is in the east
- Left – it is in the south
- Right – it is in the north.

MAKING YOUR OWN COMPASS

You should carry your compass with you at all times when travelling, secure in a rucksack pocket or on a lanyard around your neck – each member of a group should have their own compass. It is a good idea to carry a small backup compass too. However, accidents can happen – you may lose your compass or damage it, or find yourself in an emergency situation without one. At times like these, it may still be possible to put together an emergency compass.

Any long, thin and light-weight piece of ferrous metal (ie iron or steel) will serve as a makeshift compass needle – a sewing needle is ideal, but a straightened paper clip or the steel pocket clip from a pen will do, if you don't have a needle. Once you have found a suitable needle, you will then need to magnetize it.

In order to use the magnetized needle, it must be allowed to rotate freely. You can do this by suspending it on a length of sewing cotton, but this is usually impractical in the

A makeshift compass

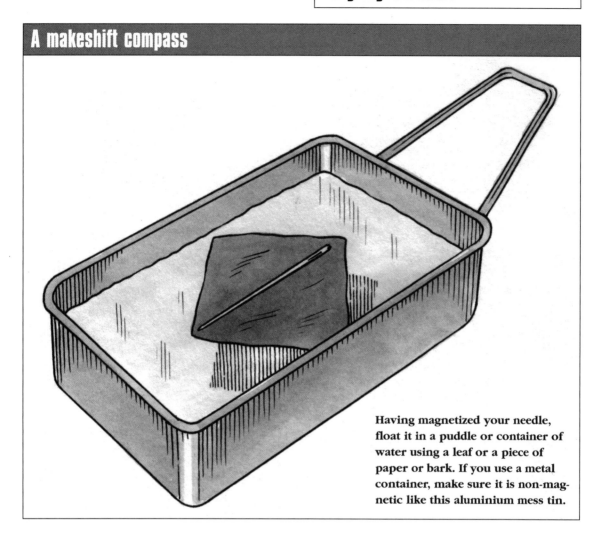

Having magnetized your needle, float it in a puddle or container of water using a leaf or a piece of paper or bark. If you use a metal container, make sure it is non-magnetic like this aluminium mess tin.

outdoors. A better method is to float the needle on water. The water can be held in a mess tin, coffee mug or other container (which must be made of non-ferrous material, eg aluminium or plastic), in a scrape in the ground or in a hollow in a rock. Place the needle on a scrap of paper, a leaf, a blade of grass or a piece of bark, and carefully float it on the water. It should rotate slowly, then settle in one direction.

To make sure that your emergency compass is working, disturb the needle a few times and check that it always returns to the same position. If it doesn't, then give it some more magnetizing strokes.

Once the needle has settled in one direction, it will be aligned north–south. But which end of the needle points north? You will have to use natural indicators – the sun is the obvious one – to decide whether the marked end of the needle is pointing north or south.

It is not possible to follow a precise compass course by holding a makeshift device like this in your hands, but at least you can stop regularly to set it up and check your general direction of travel.

ESTIMATING ANGLES AND DISTANCES

It is possible to make a rough estimate of angles by sighting along your hand. Hold your thumb up at arms length and sight along it – it covers an angle of roughly two degrees. If you want to prove this to yourself, do a bit of simple trigonometry. Get a friend to take a tape measure and measure the distance between your thumb and your eye – for example, 60cm (2ft) – and then measure the width of your thumb – 2cm (0.75in). This gives you an isosceles triangle with base of 2cm (0.75in) and a height of 60cm (2ft). The angle at your eye is therefore 2 x (inverse tangent $\frac{1}{60}$) = 1.9°.

Roughly speaking, each finger held at arm's length covers about 2° of sky or horizon. Your clenched fist covers around 8°, your splayed thumb and forefinger 15°, and your hand span from thumb to little finger 20°.

This 'rule of thumb' can be used to estimate your distance from an object of known width or height, or from two objects if you know the distance between them (in metres/feet), using the following formula:

width or separation in metres/feet/(100 x angle) = distance away in miles

If your map indicates that

Estimating angles by eye

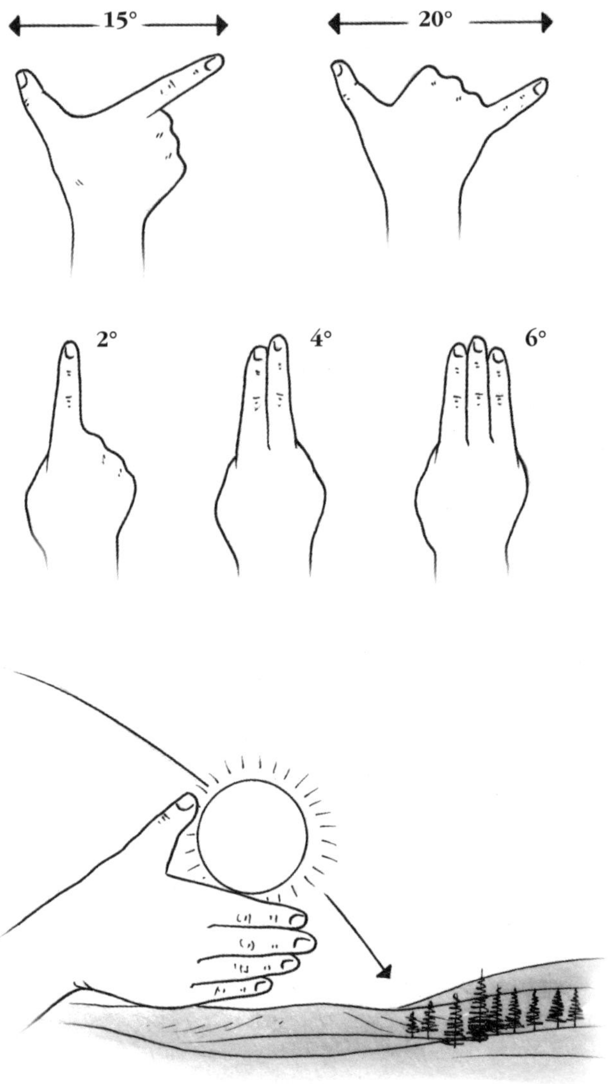

A hand held at arm's length provides a useful way of estimating the angles between distant objects. One finger covers about 2°, two fingers 4°, and so on. The span from thumb to forefinger subtends about 15°, and from thumb to little finger about 20°. One useful application of this method is in estimating the time remaining until sunset in the middle latitudes. Each finger's width above the horizon equates to about 15 minutes; in the example shown here, there is an hour left until sunset.

Distance to the horizon

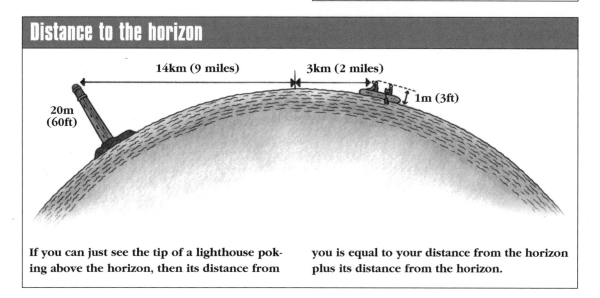

14km (9 miles)

3km (2 miles)

20m (60ft)

1m (3ft)

If you can just see the tip of a lighthouse poking above the horizon, then its distance from you is equal to your distance from the horizon plus its distance from the horizon.

the twin summits of the peak you are heading towards are 1.6km (1 mile/5280 feet) apart, and sighting along your hand shows them to be three finger-widths (ie 6° apart, then the formula (5280 / 100 x 6 = 8.8) tells you that you still have almost 14km (9 miles) to go.

DISTANCE TO THE HORIZON

The distance to the visible horizon, whether at sea, on a large lake or on a flat landscape depends on the height of your eye. Standing on a flat desert pan, with your eyes about 2m (6ft) above ground level, the horizon will be about 6km (3.3 miles) distant. If you are sitting in a canoe, with your eyes about 1m (3ft) above water level, then the distance to the horizon is just under 4km (2.5 miles).

Of course, you will be able to see things further away than that if they are tall enough. A lighthouse that stands 20m (60ft) above sea level has a horizon that is 17km (9.3 nautical miles) distant. You can add this to your own horizon, so that you would begin to see the top of the lighthouse peeking over the horizon at a distance of around 22km (12 nautical miles).

Nautical almanacs publish tables showing the distance of the horizon for various heights of eye. If you don't have one, however, as a rough approximation, the distance to the horizon (in metres/miles) is equal to the square root of your height of eye (in metres/feet).

CHAPTER FIVE

Wilderness Route-finding

Navigation is the art and science of not getting lost. Route-finding is about putting your navigational knowledge to practical use by choosing the fastest and safest way to get from A to B.

Navigation is the practice of monitoring your position and shaping your course using a map and compass. However, a pencil line drawn on the map tends to ignore the realities of the terrain. Route-finding involves picking a feasible route through and around any obstacles that might lie in the path of your chosen course, as well as allowing for the effects of any possible errors or inaccuracies when using a compass.

Your choice of route should take into consideration not only the terrain but also the likely weather conditions. For example, if you are crossing an area with many streams, and the weather forecast is for rain, you will have to think about crossing those streams. Are there any bridges? If so, will you have to make a detour from your route to find them? If there are no bridges, where will you be able to ford the streams? Will they be completely impassable after heavy rain?

Route-finding takes into account the fact that the fastest or easiest route between two points is not necessarily the most direct. This simple fact forms the basis of the sport of orienteering, in which competitors must complete a course by navigating between checkpoints as quickly as possible, choosing whichever route they consider will be the quickest.

In the illustration opposite, the shortest route between A and B is the straight-line route, but in both cases it may well be faster and easier to contour around the slope. In addition, the ridge in Fig. 1 may be lined with crags and boulders, and the bottom of the valley in Fig. 2 could be choked with thick bushes or blocked by an impassable stream.

When planning your route on the map, take such factors into consideration and think about whether a straight-line course is desirable, or indeed feasible.

READING THE TERRAIN

In order to choose the best route to your objective, you need knowledge of the terrain that you will have to cover. The best source of such knowledge is previous experience of travelling in that area, but on most occasions you will have to rely on what you can see up ahead, in addition to any information you can obtain from your map.

This is where good map-reading skills are essential. The ability to read the terrain from the shape of the contours printed on the map is one of the most useful route-finding skills you can develop. You will eventually reach the stage where relating the pattern of contours on the map to the landscape around you becomes second nature.

CONTOURS

Contours (see Chapter One) are lines that connect points of equal elevation. The spacing and form of the contours on a map reflect the shape of the landscape that they represent.

SLOPES

The distance between contours is proportional to the gradient of the slope. Obviously, you will prefer to avoid slopes that are steep enough to make walking overly strenuous or difficult (Chapter One explains how to calculate gradient).

● Widely spaced contours signify gentle slopes
● Closely spaced contours signify steep slopes
● An area without contours signifies level ground
● Several contours running together into a single line signify a vertical cliff.

SHAPES

The shapes of the contours reveal the form of the landscape. Contours with sharp angles reflect angular ridges and valleys; smooth, rounded contours reflect smooth, rounded hills.

● V-shaped contours mean a sharp spur or narrow, V-shaped valley.
● U-shaped contours mean a rounded spur or broad, U-shaped valley.
● In areas with sufficient rainfall, the map will probably show a stream or river in the floor of a valley; otherwise, check the contour heights to tell ridge and valley apart.
● Straight, parallel contours mean a straight and even hillside.
● Concentric contours of increasing height mean a hill or mountain; the summit is usually marked with a spot height.

When choosing a route through a region without roads or trails, look for valleys with level floors, easy-angle slopes and rounded ridges.

SLOPE ASPECT

Slope aspect is simply the direction in which a slope faces. You can measure the aspect of

Contouring

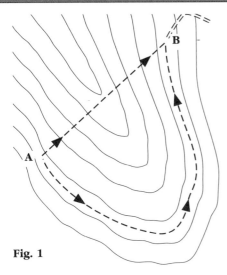

Fig. 1

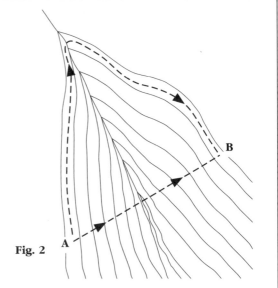

Fig. 2

Contouring means following the contour lines on a map to travel around a spur or valley without gaining or losing any height. Although it covers a longer distance, contouring is often faster and easier than taking the more direct, but steeper, route.

a slope on a map by taking a bearing that points downhill at right angles to the contours, and measure it in the field by taking a bearing facing dowhhill.

Checking the slope aspect can be useful when navigating on a mountain in poor visibility, as it can tell you on which side of the mountain you are.

NATURAL BARRIERS

Learn how your map represents landscape features that may present natural barriers, around which you will have to find a way. Make sure you can recognize features such as marshes, cliffs, gorges, steep slopes and thick forest.

Remember that maps are often unreliable when it comes to judging whether a particular barrier will prove impassable. The green area that indicates a forest may be pleasant, open woodland or a dense and impenetrable forestry plantation. This is where first-hand experience is essential.

FINDING YOUR OBJECTIVE

In theory, following a compass course should lead you straight to your objective. In the real world, however, there are many factors that conspire to throw you off course and introduce errors into the bearing you are trying to follow. Hacking through jungle, clambering over boulder fields, weaving between crags, dodging forest trees and undergrowth, detouring round lakes – the necessities of practical route-finding often make it difficult to follow a straight-line course consistently and accurately.

In addition, there is the fact that most compasses cannot be read with precision to less than 1° or 2°, and there is the possibili-

Reading contour patterns

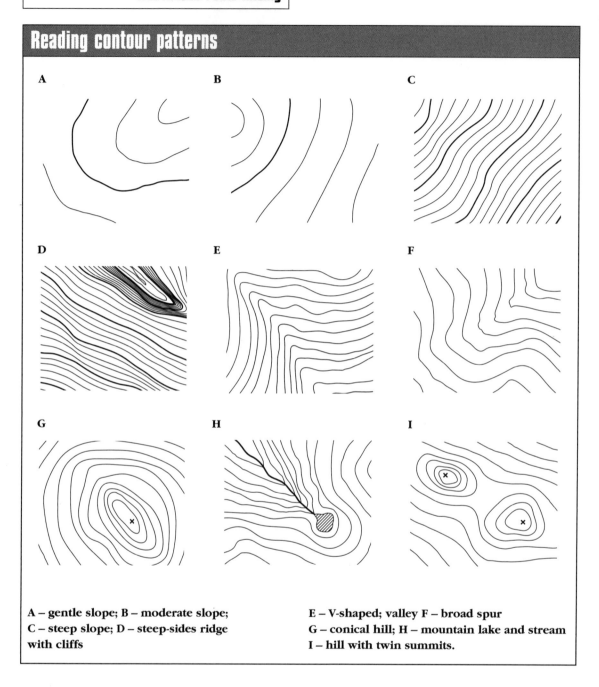

A – gentle slope; B – moderate slope;
C – steep slope; D – steep-sides ridge
with cliffs

E – V-shaped; valley F – broad spur
G – conical hill; H – mountain lake and stream
I – hill with twin summits.

ty of metal objects in your backpack introducing unnoticed deviation. If the objective you are aiming for is small and easily missed, then it makes sense to aim first for something bigger, something unmissable, that lies close to your target. You can then use the larger object to help find the smaller one.

Where mistakes are made

There are many sources of error waiting to mislead the unwary navigator.

These are the top ten causes of navigational mistakes:
- Forgetting to correct for declination
- Correcting for declination the wrong way
- Aligning the orienting arrow with the south end of the compass needle instead of the north end
- Measuring or plotting a back bearing instead of a direct bearing
- Forgetting about possible causes of deviation – do not take a compass bearing while standing next to a car
- Misreading the scale of a map
- Trying to follow a compass course without using intermediate landmarks
- Assuming that your compass bearings are more accurate than they actually are – assume an error of plus, or minus, 2°
- Forgetting to check your location on the map regularly
- Being caught by bad weather or poor visibility without an accurate position fix.

BASELINES

A baseline is simply some linear feature that forms a boundary to the area you are travelling in, or defines a limit beyond which you will know that you have overshot your objective.

The most obvious example of a baseline is a road. For example, if your trek begins at a road that runs east–west, and your hike takes you north, then you know that if you ever get lost or need to hike out in an emergency, all you have to do is head in the general direction of south and you will eventually hit the road.

BEARINGS AS BASELINES

A baseline does not have to be a physical feature. It can be an imaginary line like a transit or a bearing. For example, you are trying to find a small lake hidden in the woods. You will not be able to see the lake until you are very close to it, but there is a prominent peak nearby that is almost constantly in view. Use the map to measure the bearing of the peak from the lake; this is your baseline bearing. Let's say it is 270°.

If you then aim off (see section below) so that you will cross the baseline bearing between the lake and the peak, you can avoid overshooting the lake by regularly checking the bearing of the peak. If you are approaching from the south, the bearing of the peak from your start position might be, say, 345°. As you head north, this bearing will gradually decrease. If it falls below 270° you have gone too far. Retrace your steps until the peak bears exactly 270°, then follow the back bearing (ie 090°), which will lead you to the lake.

LIMITING BEARINGS

In the illustration overleaf, the hiker has used her map to ascertain that a bearing of 135° on the radio mast avoids the dangerous gully in the rim of the plateau. As she approaches the area of the gully, she checks the bearing of the mast. If it is 135° or less, then she knows she will pass the gully safely. If the bearing is more than 135°, then she can alter her course to the right until she returns to a safe bearing. A bearing such as this is called a limiting bearing, and is freqently used to keep away from potential hazards.

Another example is shown using a sailing boat which is entering a bay whose entrance is flanked by dangerous rocks. As the wind is

Limiting bearings

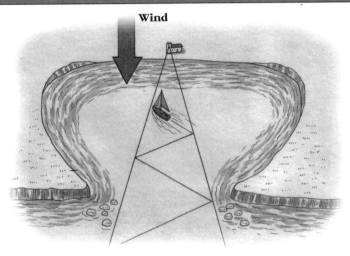

Wind

As it tacks into the bay, this sailboat is using two limiting bearings on the church to keep it clear of the rocks at the entrance.

This hiker is using a limiting bearing on the radio mast ahead to avoid getting too close to the edge of a dangerous gully.

blowing straight off the land, the boat has to tack into the bay (ie sail a zig-zag course to windward).

From the chart, the navigator has ascertained that as long as the bearing of the church on the shore remains between 340° and 020°, the boat will stay clear of the rocks. So the helmsman knows that if he keeps an eye on the bearing of the church, and tacks when it reaches 020° or 340°, the boat will be safe.

AIMING OFF

Being aware of the possibility of errors in following a course means that you can allow for those errors before they occur. Choosing a compass course towards a small target, means running the risk of missing the target – and you will not know which way to turn to find it.

Aiming off means introducing a deliberate error, so that when you miss your target, you will know on which side you have missed it. Instead of aiming directly at your target, you choose a course which leads to a baseline off to one side of your target.

In the illustration on page 91, for example, the hiker has deliberately chosen a course which hits his baseline (the river) well upstream from his target (the tent). Any small errors in following the course would still result in him arriving upstream of the target, so when he reaches the river he knows exactly which way to turn to find the camp site.

BRACKETING

Bracketing is a refinement of aiming off that involves noting landmarks along your chosen baseline that 'bracket' your objective. This means that if you arrive at the baseline and find one of the bracketing features, you will know which way to turn to find the target.

For example, let's say that your camp is beside a river (see the illustration on page 92), and the hills that you are exploring lie 3km (2 miles) away to the north. If you had to follow a compass course from the hills to your camp, then a maximum error of 5° on either side of your course could lead you to miss the camp by up to 260m (780 ft) in either direction.

As a precaution, you have explored the riverbank upstream and downstream from the camp site, noting features like the dead tree and prominent boulder to the west, and the big oak tree and ploughed field to the east.

After a day's hiking in the hills, you descend back towards camp in mist and heavy rain. Because of the poor visibility, you follow a compass course, but the inevitable errors caused by the rough terrain mean that when you reach the river there is no sign of your tent.

However, because you have been sensible enough to explore the area around your camp, and noted down bracketing features within the likely area of error, all you have to do is to turn in either direction and follow the river. If you turn left and find the dead tree or the prominent boulder, you are reassured that you are on the right track. If you turn left and find the big oak tree or the ploughed field, you know you are heading the wrong way, and will need to turn around.

Aiming off

While returning to camp, this hiker deliberately set a compass course that would lead him to the river upstream of his tent, even if he made an error of up to 5° in following the compass course. By aiming off in this manner, he can be sure of which way to turn when he reaches the river.

Aiming off in olden times

The technique of aiming off was used extensively by mariners in the days of sail. When heading for a port that lay, for example, on the coast of Africa or South America, a ship's master would head north or south until he reached a latitude that lay upwind of his destination, then sail directly east or west until the coast came into sight. Once land was sighted, the captain knew which way to turn to find the port he was looking for.

COLLECTING FEATURES

Like a baseline, a collecting feature (sometimes called a handrail) can be any linear feature in the landscape – a road, a river, a shoreline, a mountain ridge, a line of telegraph poles – but instead of using it as delimiting line, you use it as a direction indicator.

For example, if you can see from your map that a line of cliffs off to your left trends from southeast to northwest, which is parallel to the course you want to follow, you can forget about your compass for a while. As long as those cliffs are to your left, and you are travelling parallel to them, you know that you are still on course.

Man-made features often make useful collecting features. A line of electricity pylons leading over a hill pass or a railway track crossing an empty stretch of desert can act as a check on your direction. As long as you can identify the feature on the map, you can

Bracketing

Bracketing means taking note of features that lie on either side of your chosen target, so that when you reach one of the bracketing features, you will know in which direction to turn to find the target.

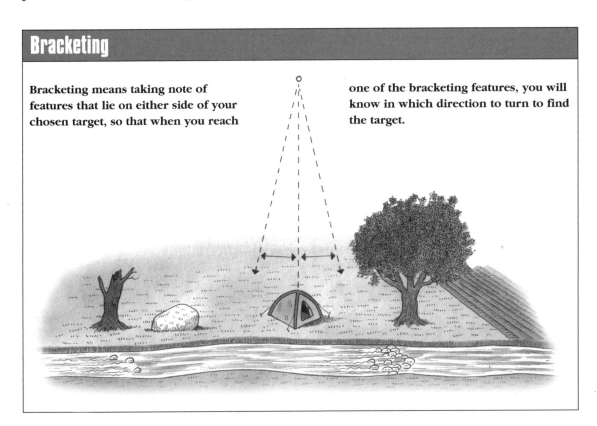

use it to keep yourself on course.

CHECK FEATURES

Check features (sometimes called catch points) are identifiable locations along a route or on a collecting feature that help you to measure your progress or pinpoint your position on the map. For example, a bridge on a river, a river-mouth on a shoreline, a rail-road crossing on a road.

You can use check features to mentally 'tick off' your progress along a route, or to remind you where to change direction to a new compass course, or you can use one as an attack point.

ATTACK POINTS

An attack point is a special type of check feature. It is an easily identifiable spot, close to your intended objective, that you can use as a starting point for homing in on your objective.

When you are trying to find some small feature whose location you know from the map, it is easier to head first for some larger feature close by – an attack point – and then close in on your target by simply following a compass course from there. If you are looking for a needle in a haystack, then it is best if you first find the haystack.

For example, if you tried to find the fishing hole in the illustration on page 94 by following a compass bearing directly to it from the road, there is a good chance that errors in keeping to a straight course would cause you to miss it.

Instead, choose the easily findable intersection of the crag and fence at A, and use

Collecting feature

A collecting feature or handrail is a linear feature in the landscape which provides a directional guide. The hiker here knows from the map that the river he can see to his north runs in an east–west direction; as long as he keeps it in view on his right-hand side, he will be travelling west.

that as an attack point. Once there, you can then follow a much shorter compass course to the fishing hole. Alternatively, you can pace along the fence to the point where it is closest to the fishing hole, and follow a compass course from there. The shorter distances between an attack point and your objective mean that there is less chance of missing it through error.

ROUTE-FINDING IN DIFFICULT TERRAIN

Mountains

Most routes in the mountains follow major valleys and ridges. In some mountain ranges, the main ridges all run in the same direction. In such places, travelling on a route parallel to the main ridges may be fairly straightforward, but attempting a route that cuts across at right angles to the trend of the range may involve a lot of tiring and time-consuming ascent and descent.

In populated mountain areas, the routes over passes and from valleys up to high pastures will have trails made over the years by the local villagers or shepherds. In uninhabited areas where the valleys are filled with dense forest and torrential rivers, you will often make better progress on the ridges above the tree line, provided they are not too narrow or blocked by crags.

When climbing steeper slopes where there is no trail, take a zig-zag route up the hillside – this is much easier than heading straight up the slope.

Scree slopes

Scree, or talus, is an accumulation of small, loose stones that builds up at the foot of a cliff or gully. Scree slopes generally lie at an angle of around 20° to 30°, which is steep enough to make uphill walking difficult. Scree also provides a very insecure footing, with the loosely piled stones sliding down as soon as you put weight on them. This makes for extremely strenuous and tiring progress. Consequently, if at all possible, avoid any route that involves climbing a scree slope.

On the other hand, scree slopes can make for very fast and easy descents, provided the size of the stones is small enough. Scree-running involves descending in big, exaggerated steps, with your weight on your heels. Beware of sending stones cascading down on anyone who might be below, and do not run down a scree slope if you cannot see the bottom of it; it may run out over a cliff.

Mountain streams

Mountain streams are usually much more vigorous and violent than lowland ones, with steep gradients, fast-flowing currents and many waterfalls. They erode steep-sided, V-shaped valleys, and their banks are often dangerously unstable. Crossing such streams can be impossible without a bridge.

In mountains which receive considerable snow-fall, the spring thaw sends torrents of water down these valleys, making them impassable at that time of year. Severe erosion can obliterate last year's trails, and even roads can be washed away.

Attack points

An attack point is an easily identifiable location that can be used as a starting point for closing in on a hard-to-find target. It is easier to find the little lake by using the wall as an attack point, rather than trying to follow a direct compass course from road to lake.

Avalanche danger

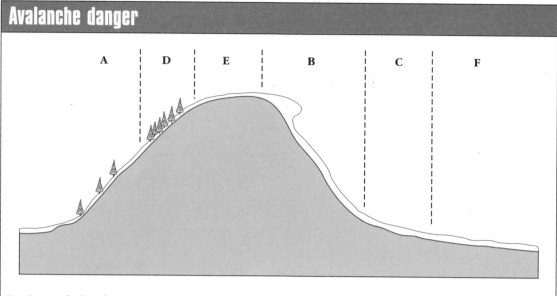

During and after heavy snowfall there is a danger of avalanche, especially on moderate open slopes (A), steep downwind slopes (B) and the areas beneath them (C). Safer areas include densely forested slopes (D), ridge crests (E) and the middle of broad valley floors (F). Danger is at a maximum during and immediately after heavy snowfall.

When planning a route in such areas, take into account the location and frequency of bridges; do not assume that you will be able to ford mountain streams.

Avalanche areas

When moving through snow-covered mountains in winter, you should be aware of the potential danger from avalanches. The most likely time for an avalanche to occur is during or after a heavy snowfall, but certain slopes are more avalanche-prone than others and you should bear this in mind when planning a route.

The most dangerous areas are steep, downwind slopes, where drifted snow piles up, and the gentler slopes and valley floors below them, which are threatened by avalanches from higher up. Steep gullies which can funnel avalanche debris are also dangerous.

The safest places are the crests of ridges, slopes with dense forest, and the central parts of wide valley floors. However, beware of cornices on ridges – venture too close to one of these overhanging snow-crests and it could collapse. Keep to the upwind side of the ridge.

Remember that the most common trigger for avalanches that kill people are the people themselves. Never try to cross a slope that you suspect of being avalanche prone.

Glaciers

Glaciers are rivers of ice that are common in high mountains all over the world, and in polar regions, such as Greenland and Antarctica. Glaciers can often provide a relatively easy route into the heart of a mountain range as long as you can avoid the danger of crevasses.

Crevasses are large, deep cracks in the surface of a glacier. They form where the

Using an altimeter

If the safe route down a mountain involves following a ridge, then descending to one side of the crest to avoid a steep or rocky section, an altimeter can alert you to the proper point to leave the ridge when visibility is poor. Set the altimeter to the correct height at the summit, and note from the map the height at the top of the steep section; keep an eye on the altimeter reading, and leave the ridge before you reach the noted height.

glacier experiences a change in slope or direction, and are at their most dangerous in winter and spring when they are concealed by a thick covering of snow.

The easiest and safest part of a glacier is usually on a moraine. A moraine is a ridge of rocks, boulders and gravel that has been scraped up and carried along by the glacier. There are lateral moraines at either side of the glacier, and where two glaciers join together they may form a medial moraine below the confluence.

The trails that lead from the high valleys to mountaineering expdition base camps in the Himalayas often lead along moraines.

Polar regions

The polar regions are defined as the areas of the planet that lie north of 66.5° N and south of 66.5° S. In addition to the physical difficulties of low temperatures, bad weather and travelling over snow and ice, there are potential navigational problems to be considered in some places.

Magnetic compasses are unreliable in areas close to the magnetic poles; use the sun and stars to keep a check on direction. Also, if you venture onto the Arctic sea ice, remember that the ice itself is drifting, introducing errors into your dead reckoning (see Chapter Three). It is well worth investing in a GPS receiver for travel in the polar regions.

Desert

A desert is defined as a region that receives less than 250mm (10in) of precipitation a year. Hot deserts cover around a fifth of the earth's land surface and lie mostly in the region of the tropics. The world's main desert areas include the Sahara in northern Africa; the Kalahari in southern Africa; the Arabian desert; central and western Australia; southwestern USA and northern Mexico; and the Atacama desert in Chile and Peru.

The main challenge to travellers in desert regions is coping with extreme temperatures and lack of natural water sources. It is usually best to find shade and rest up during the middle of the day, and do most of your travelling in the morning, late afternoon and night. Carry sufficient water to last between water sources, plus emergency rations.

Mirages

In desert regions, the sun's heat warms up the ground, and the ground in turn heats up the layer of air immediately above it. In flat areas of desert this layer of hot air close to the ground behaves like a lens and refracts light, producing a mirage.

A mirage is an optical illusion. The horizon is obscured by what looks like a pale, shimmering surface (which can be mistaken for a lake or the sea), and it may be possible to see mountains which would normally be invisible beyond the horizon. This effect can be very confusing, as it is difficult to make out the true shape of the landscape, and it makes taking accurate bearings of landmarks almost impossible.

If you can manage to find a rock outcrop or a hill that projects more than 3m (10ft) above the general ground level, you may be able to climb above the layer of air that is causing the mirage and get a clearer view of your surroundings.

Jungles and forests

Because of the sheer volume of trees and dense undergrowth, tropical jungle and forest can prove a real challenge to the navigator. You may have to travel for long distances without getting a good view of any landmarks that would allow you to ascertain your position. A thick forest canopy can also obscure the sun and the stars so that you have to rely entirely on your compass for direction. Equatorial rain forest is thick enough to prevent a handheld GPS receiver from getting a reliable fix.

In forest regions with navigable rivers and lakes, such as the Amazon basin and northwest Canada, the traditional way to travel has always been by canoe. If you are travelling on foot, then following a trail, either human or animal, is your best option. Carry your compass in your hand and check your direction frequently. If you are venturing into unknown territory, use dead reckoning (see Chapter Three) to keep track of your progress.

Forestry roads

Commerical forestry plantations and logging areas can also prove difficult. Forestry roads change frequently as logging operations progress, and only a very recent map will show them with any degree of accuracy. It is, however, easier to follow a road (keeping a close eye on its direction using your compass) the long way round rather than attempt to carry on directly through the trees.

In tropical jungle you may have to hack a route through untracked forest. This can slow your progress to less than 1.5km (1 mile) an hour. When using a machete, chop diagonally downward and aim to hit the vegetation as low down as possible, so that it falls away from your trail and not across it.

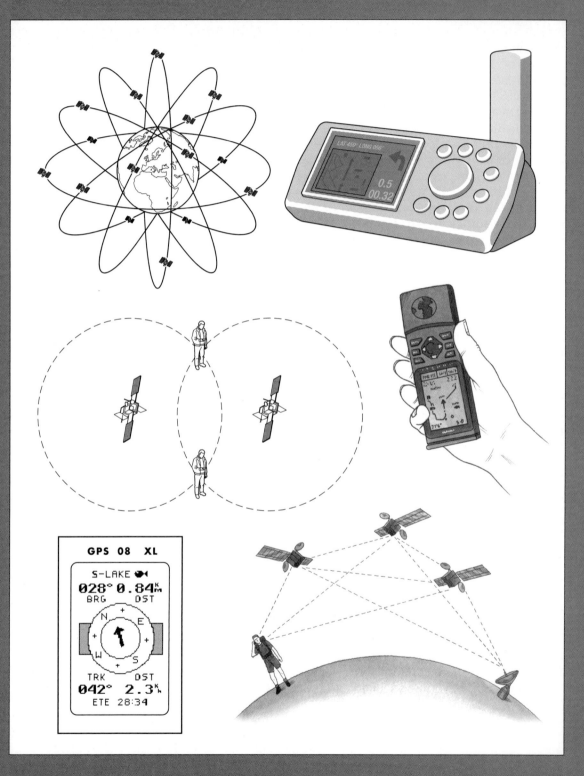

CHAPTER SIX

Using Handheld GPS

The Global Positioning System (GPS) has revolutionized navigation. A handheld GPS receiver the size and cost of a mobile phone can tell you exactly where you are, anywhere in the world, to the nearest 15m (50ft), or better.

The widespread availability of affordable GPS receivers since the mid-1990s has brought about a revolution in outdoor navigation. Their accuracy and ability to function in all weathers has brought a huge safety benefit to many people engaged in outdoor activities.

GPS technology is improving and becoming cheaper all the time, and in the near future you can expect to see miniaturized GPS receivers installed in mobile phones, handheld PCs, and many other electronic devices.

THE GLOBAL POSITIONING SYSTEM

GPS was the brainchild of the US Department of Defense, and was intended to provide precise and reliable all-weather navigation for the US Army, Navy, and Air force. Development of the system began in the early 1970s, but it did not become fully operational until the mid-1990s. The project was originally known as Navstar GPS (for Navigation Satellite Timing and Ranging Global Positioning System), but is now universally referred to simply as GPS.

As with many items of military technology before it, GPS quickly proved to have numerous civilian applications, including mapping, surveying, geodesy, as well as commercial and recreational navigation.

THE SYSTEM

The GPS navigation system consists of three separate parts: the control segment, the space segment and the user segment.

CONTROL SEGMENT

The control segment consists of five ground stations located at US Air Force bases around the world in Colorado Springs (continental USA); Hawaii (mid-Pacific Ocean); Ascension Island (south Atlantic Ocean); Diego Garcia (Indian Ocean); and Kwajalein (western Pacific). The ground stations continuously monitor the satellites, tracking their exact positions, adjusting their orbits, keeping their atomic clocks synchronized, and transmitting precise location and timing data back to the satellites.

SPACE SEGMENT

A total of 24 GPS satellites orbit the earth at an altitude of around 20,200km (12,625 miles). There are six orbital planes, with four satellites in each plane (see the illustration on page 101), and each satellite makes one complete orbit every 12 hours. The orbits are arranged so that at all times at least five satellites are in view from any point on the earth's surface.

Each satellite continuously transmits radio signals which contain coded data

describing its location and speed, and the location and speed of all the other satellites. It also transmits the exact time as given by its atomic clocks.

The satellites all talk to one another, so that each satellite knows where all the others are at any given time.

USER SEGMENT

The user segment consists of all the GPS receivers in the world. Because all a GPS receiver requires to fix its position is to receive the signals transmitted by the satellites – a GPS unit does not transmit – there is no upper limit on the number of users.

WHY USE GPS?

The advantages of a handheld GPS receiver over traditional navigational techniques are many. It works 24 hours a day in all weathers, in all parts of the world, and can fix your position to within 15m (50ft) – sufficiently precise to tell which side of a river you are standing on.

The GPS receiver has three main factors that make it useful to the wilderness navigator. It will:

● Fix your position accurately and precisely, even in zero visibility

Atomic clock precision

Without the extreme precision provided by atomic clocks, GPS would not work. The precision of a GPS position depends on the precision of the measurements of the time taken for radio signals travelling at the speed of light (around 300,000km/sec, or 186,000miles/sec) to travel from satellite to receiver. An error of 1 millisecond (one thousandth of a second) in the timing would result in an error of 320km (200 miles) in the position. Atomic clocks allow this timing to be measured with a precision calculated in nanoseconds (billionths of a second).

GPS satellite constellation

The Global Positioning System consists of 24 satellites orbiting the earth at a height of 20,200km (12,625 miles). Each satellite takes 12 hours to make a complete orbit.

the simple reason that a GPS receiver is an electronic device which can malfunction, become damaged, or get lost. Its batteries can also go flat, rendering it useless.

In addition, unless you have an expensive receiver that can display electronic maps, you will still need a paper map to plot and keep track of your position. Also, if you keep the receiver switched on permanently, the batteries will last no longer than 24 hours or so. This means that on a multi-day trip, unless you are prepared to lug several sets of batteries around, you cannot expect to keep the unit on constantly.

For most outdoor pursuits, therefore, a GPS receiver is used only occasionally to check the accuracy of your position, while most of the time you will be using traditional methods of navigation. This saves the battery power for emergencies, when GPS really comes into its own.

GPS depends on the clear reception of radio signals, so a GPS receiver will

● Tell you what direction your objective lies in, and how far away it is
● Remember your current position so that you can find your way back to it.

LIMITATIONS OF GPS

Considering its accuracy and convenience, the question in the previous section might be better phrased as 'Why not use GPS?'. Despite its advantages, GPS should never be relied upon as your only navigational tool, for

not function properly anywhere that the radio signals are blocked or where reception is poor. Places where GPS will normally not work at all include:

● Inside a building
● In a cave
● Underwater.

Places where reception may be poor or patchy include:

GPS signal reception

In certain places a GPS receiver may not be able to get a clear satellite signal and will therefore provide an inaccurate position. Such places include cities with tall buildings, dense forest or jungle, and deep gorges. In such areas it may be necessary to stop and climb to a higher location in order to get enough satellite signals to fix your position accurately.

- On a city street, surrounded by tall buildings
- In a deep gorge, or steep-sided valley
- In dense jungle or forest

SOURCES OF ERROR

There are various factors which may introduce errors into a GPS position fix. Most of these affect the radio signals on their journey between satellite and receiver and are described below. Other errors are introduced by slight inaccuracies in the satellites' atomic clocks, and by variations in the tracking of the satellites' exact orbital paths.

IONOSPHERIC INTERFERENCE

As a radio signal passes through the charged particles of the ionosphere (the region of the earth's atmosphere extending about 60–1000km (40–625 miles), above the surface of the earth) and then the clouds of water vapour in the troposphere below, it is refracted. This introduces slight timing errors because the signal follows a path that is slightly longer than a straight line. Ionospheric interference can be dealt with in two ways:

- Error modelling
- Dual frequency measurement.

Error modelling uses a mathematical model to predict what the typical error caused by the ionosphere and troposphere will be on a typical day, and applies a suitable correction. Civilian receivers use this method.

The dual frequency method is more accurate, and is used by military receivers. It takes advantage of the fact that radio signals of different frequencies are refracted by different amounts. By measuring the difference in timing of two signals of different frequency, the precise effect of refraction can be calculated.

GPS satellites transmit their signals on two frequencies, called L1 and L2. Civilian receivers can pick up L1 only, but military receivers detect both, allowing them to apply the dual frequency correction.

SATELLITE GEOMETRY

When obtaining a position fix using two intersecting compass bearings, the potential error is reduced when the two bearings are at roughly 90° to one another (see Chapter Three). Similarly, there is an ideal geometry for the locations of the four satellites required to produce an accurate position fix using GPS.

Satellite geometry, also known as satellite constellation, refers to the pattern of satellites visible to a GPS receiver at the time it is calculating its position. The ideal geometry has one satellite overhead and another three evenly spaced around the horizon.

When a GPS receiver is switched on, it begins by scanning the sky to see which satellites are visible. Usually, there are more satellites available than the four needed to fix a position, so it chooses the four with the best geometry and ignores the rest. However, if high mountains or buildings are blocking part of the sky, then it has to make do with those that are visible, which may not have an ideal geometry.

In such cases, a potential error called Geometric Dilution of Precision (GDOP) may be introduced. This is the GPS equivalent of two bearings at a shallow angle producing a potential error when fixing your position using compass bearings (see Chapter Three).

MULTIPATH ERROR

In the final stages of its journey from satellite to receiver, the radio signal may be reflected from cliffs, mountains, buildings or other high structures. This means that the receiver may pick up the same signal two or more times – once directly from the satellite, and then from the various reflections. This produces an error called

The Global Positioning System

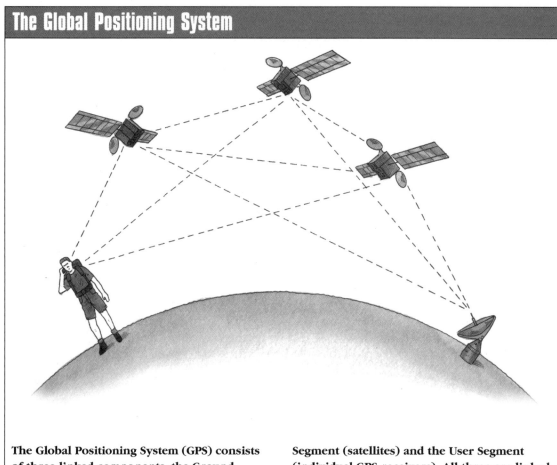

The Global Positioning System (GPS) consists of three linked components: the Ground Segment (ground control stations), the Space Segment (satellites) and the User Segment (individual GPS receivers). All three are linked by continuous radio transmissions.

multipath error; a similar effect causes 'ghosting' on TV screens when the aerial is positioned where it picks up a reflected signal from nearby buildings. Most GPS receivers cannot correct for multipath error, so be aware of features around you that may cause it.

SELECTIVE AVAILABILITY

You may have heard the term 'Selective Availability' (SA) used in relation to GPS. When GPS was first made available to civilians, the US Department of Defense maintained a military advantage by introducing a deliberate and random error into the signals used by civilian receivers. The system was called Selective Availability.

This meant that while military receivers could obtain positions to within 15m (50ft), and in some cases to within 1m (3ft) or less, civilian receivers were only accurate to within 100m (330ft); the actual amount of error was random and unknowable. However, SA was removed on 1 May 2000, and civilian receivers are now able to match the accuracy of military receivers.

Satellite geometry

Satellite geometry refers to the pattern of satellites in the sky around a GPS receiver as it computes a position. The ideal geometry consists of one satellite overhead and three others spaced evenly around the horizon. The receiver chooses the best geometry from available satellites.

HOW GPS WORKS

Despite its use of technology, GPS is based on the same navigational principle of resection that was described in Chapter Three to fix a position using intersecting compass bearings.

A compass allows you to measure the bearing from a point of known location to give you a position line. A GPS receiver measures the distance from a point of known location to give a position sphere. Just as two compass bearings intersect at a unique position on the earth's surface, so do three position spheres.

MEASURING TIME AND DISTANCE

Radio waves travel at the speed of light, which is approximately 300,000km/sec (186,000miles/sec). A GPS receiver measures the distance between it and a satellite by measuring the time it takes for a radio signal to travel between them, and then multiplies this by the speed of light. The equation is:

● velocity x time = distance

For example, if you know that a car is travelling at a constant speed, you can find out the

GPS error budget

This table shows the contribution made by various sources of error to the typical accuracy of a GPS position fix:

Source of error	Contribution to total error
Satellite clocks	1.5m (5ft)
Orbit errors	2.5m (8ft)
Ionosphere	5.0m (16ft)
Troposphere	0.5m (1.6ft)
Multipath error	0.5m (1.6ft)

Typical accuracy 10m (33ft)

distance between two points on the road by measuring the time it takes for the car to travel between them. If the car's speed is 100km/h (60mph), and the time taken is 30 minutes (ie 0.5 hours), then the distance between the two points must be 0.5 x 100 = 50km (30miles).

But how do you measure the travel time of a radio signal? Consider the following analogy, using sound waves instead of radio waves. We are all familiar with the time lapse between seeing something happen in the distance and hearing it. For example, there is a delay between seeing a flash of lightning and hearing the associated thunder. Indeed, we sometimes calculate how far away the lightning is by counting the seconds between flash and rumble. The speed of sound is around 330m (1083ft)/sec, so a three second gap would mean that the lightning was about 1km (0.6 mile) away (330 x 3 = 990m).

We can carry out this calculation because we know exactly when to start counting – the lightning flash, and our perception of it, are synchronous, and effectively simultaneous.

Imagine that instead of lightning, someone starts broadcasting a piece of music on a continuous loop of tape over a huge sound system at exactly 12 noon. You are within hearing range, but you do not know exactly how far away. If your watch was synchronized exactly with that person's watch, you could start playing the same continuous loop of music at exactly the same time. There would then be a delay between your own music and the incoming music, that could be measured at any time by delaying your own music until it fell into synch with the incoming music. This time delay could then be used to calculate the distance to the broadcaster.

This is the principle used by GPS receivers. Instead of music, the satellite broadcasts a 'pseudo random code', basically a sequence of coded numbers. The receiver, whose internal clock is exactly synchronized with the satellite clocks, compares the timing of the sequence, calculates the delay and multiplies it by the speed of light to give the distance.

SYNCHRONIZING CLOCK TIMES

The average time taken for a radio signal to travel from satellite to receiver is around 0.06 seconds. This is why the extremely high level of precision provided by atomic clocks in necessary for GPS to function.

Atomic clocks cost in the region of US$50,000–100,000 – evidently, your US$100 GPS receiver does not contain one. However, by using a clever mathematical trick during the position-fixing process, a GPS receiver can synchronize its internal clock with the satellite clocks, giving it the necessary atomic-clock accuracy.

SATELLITE LOCATION

So we know how a GPS receiver can calculate the distance between itself and the satellite.

Position fixing – one satellite

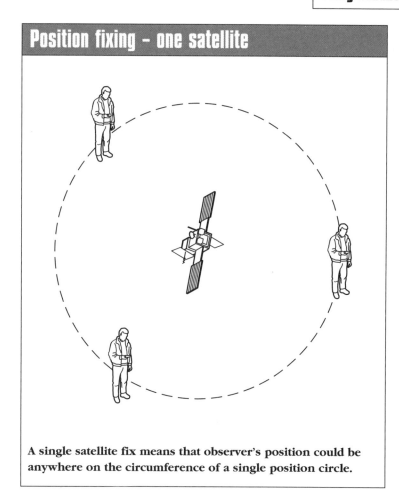

A single satellite fix means that observer's position could be anywhere on the circumference of a single position circle.

corrections are transmitted to the satellites every hour or so. Each time a GPS receiver connects with a satellite, its first action is to download the latest ephemeris data and update its almanac.

GPS POSITION FIXING

Once the GPS receiver knows the exact location and distance of a satellite, it can draw a position sphere around that particular point – the receiver must lie somewhere on the surface of that sphere. In reality, of course, it could not be just anywhere on that sphere as most of it is out in space. It is more likely to lie somewhere on or close to the surface of the earth; GPS positions are three-dimensional, and include altitude.

A simplified illustration of how a GPS receiver fixes its position is shown in the diagrams on pages 107–109 – assume that the circles shown are the intersection of the satellite position spheres with the surface of the earth.

With a single satellite, we have a one position circle – the receiver could lie anywhere on its circumference (see above left). With two satellites we have two intersecting position circles, so the receiver's position has been narrowed down to one of two points (page 108). The addition of a third satellite provides a third position circle, which fixes the position of the receiver at an unambiguous point (page 109).

In reality, the intersection of three spheres gives two points rather than one.

But how does it know the exact location of the satellite, which is whizzing along at 2200km/h (1375mph), about 20,200km (12,625 miles) above the earth?

The answer is that the radio signal broadcast by the satellite contains information about the satellite's position and speed, as well as the pseudo random code used for timing. This information is known as the 'ephemeris data', and it is stored in an almanac program in the receiver that allows it to calculate the exact position of any satellite at any given time.

The ephemeris data are continuously monitored by GPS ground stations, and any

Position fixing – two satellites

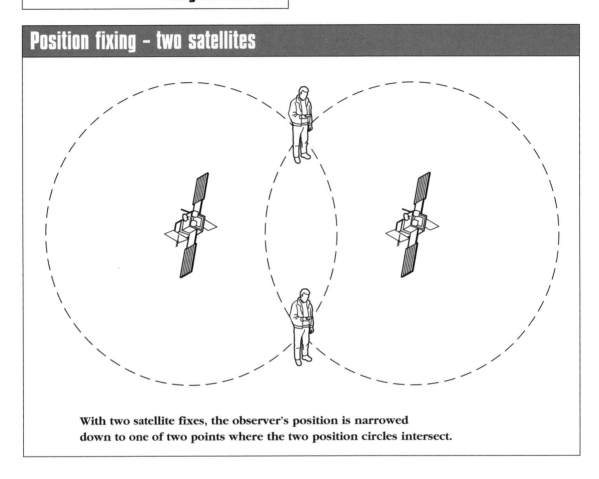

**With two satellite fixes, the observer's position is narrowed
down to one of two points where the two position circles intersect.**

However, the receiver can easily tell that one of these points is far out in space and simply discards it.

The signal from a fourth satellite is needed in order to synchronize the receiver's internal clock with the satellites' atomic clocks, so a minimum of four satellites is required to provide an accurate fix.

2D MODE

When the receiver's view of the sky is limited, it may only be able to lock on to three satellites. In this case it still needs to use one satellite to synchronize its clock; it then drops the altitude calculation and uses the other two signals to give a two-dimensional (2D) position.

When this happens, the receiver will display a symbol indicating that it is functioning in 2D mode. The position error that is generated in 2D mode can range from 150–1525m (500–5000ft), so try not to rely too closely on 2D positions. If possible, change your location so that the receiver has a clearer view of the sky.

GPS RECEIVERS

There is a huge range of GPS receivers on the market, ranging from pocket-sized hand-held units to the large, computer-integrated receivers used on commercial ships and aircraft. There are GPS units specially designed for use by hikers, sailors, car drivers, anglers, fishermen, pilots, surveyors and scientists.

Position fixing – three satellites

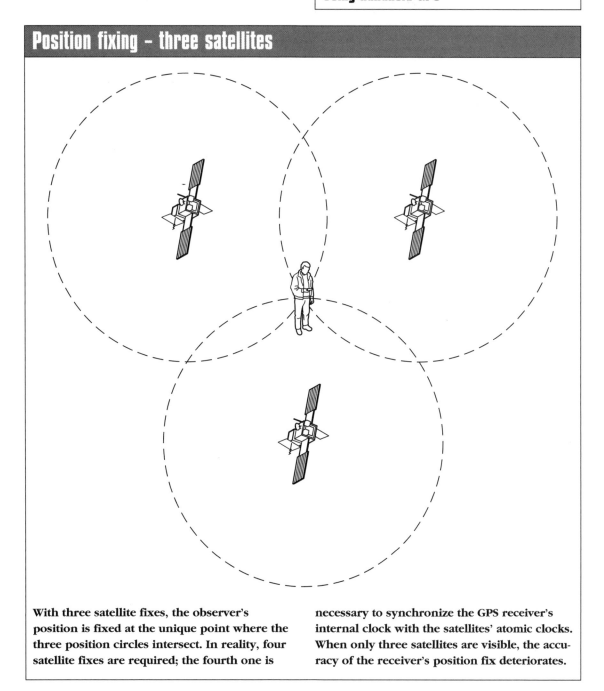

With three satellite fixes, the observer's position is fixed at the unique point where the three position circles intersect. In reality, four satellite fixes are required; the fourth one is necessary to synchronize the GPS receiver's internal clock with the satellites' atomic clocks. When only three satellites are visible, the accuracy of the receiver's position fix deteriorates.

This section will concentrate on handheld receivers designed for use by people engaged in outdoor sports.

The latest handheld models are about the same size and weight as a mobile phone, and not that much more expensive; the cheapest models sell for around US$100. There is even a wristwatch-mounted GPS.

All GPS units manufactured since 1998 have parallel channels, allowing them to track and read data from up to 12 satellites at a time.

Some older receivers (known as multiplexing receivers) have a single channel, which samples the data from each satellite in turn. These are a little less reliable when moving through dense forest or steep-sided valleys, where trees or terrain may momentarily block the satellite signal.

NON-MAPPING UNITS

A non-mapping unit displays navigational information in the form of a set of coordinates which must be plotted on or compared with a map. It will also have the standard navigation screens showing the bearing and distance to a selected waypoint (see Features section below).

MAPPING UNITS

The more expensive mapping unit stores one or more electronic maps in its memory, and can display a map directly on its screen with your position shown correctly on it. Mapping units also give the option of using standard navigation screens found on non-mapping receivers.

MULTI-NAVIGATORS

Some manufacturers, including Brunton and Silva, have produced what they call a multi-navigator, which combines a GPS receiver with an electronic compass, altimeter and barometer, all in the same device. The electronic compass uses very little battery power, and is best used like a normal compass to navigate between waypoints, only occasionally switching on the GPS unit to check on your exact position.

GPS AND PDAs

There has been a huge rise in the ownership of handheld computers (also known as personal digital assistants, or PDAs) in the last decade. These devices are small and light and provide an impressive amount of computing power. Although they were originally designed as the electronic equivalent of diaries and address books, PDAs are now capable of all kinds of complex computing tasks, including navigation.

Handheld computers using Microsoft's Windows CE operating system (OS), known as Pocket PCs, and the more widespread Palm devices can both be used with a miniaturized GPS receiver, which is available as an accessory. Electronic maps can be downloaded from CDs or the Internet and installed on the handheld computer, whose high-resolution colour display can then provide all the advantages of a larger and more expensive GPS mapping unit. The most obvious of these is the ability to show your position directly on an electronic map on the PDA's display, instead of a grid reference that has to be plotted on a paper map or chart.

GPS FEATURES

Listed here are some of the basic features

Manufacturers of handheld GPS receivers

The following are the websites of the main manufacturers of handheld GPS receivers for outdoor sports:

Brunton: www.brunton.com
Garmin: www.garmin.com
Lowrance: www.lowrance.com
Magellan: www.magellangps.com
Silva: www.silva.se

A handheld GPS receiver

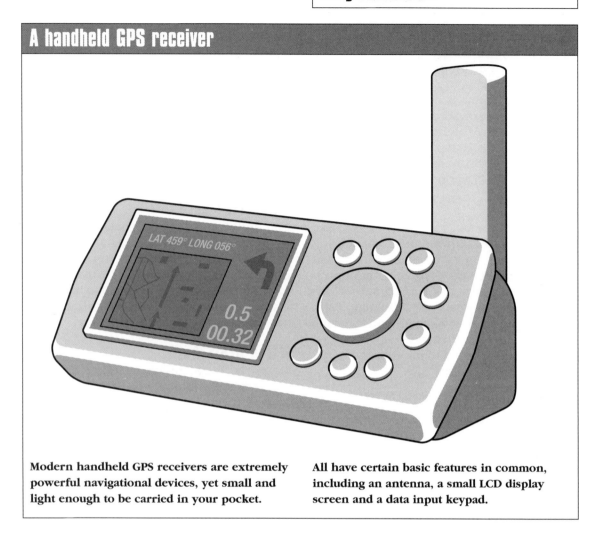

Modern handheld GPS receivers are extremely powerful navigational devices, yet small and light enough to be carried in your pocket.

All have certain basic features in common, including an antenna, a small LCD display screen and a data input keypad.

that should be considered when choosing and using a GPS receiver.

ANTENNA

The antenna, or aerial, is the part of the receiver that picks up the radio signal from the satellite. The highest quality GPS receivers have a separate antenna, connected by a cable, which can be placed high up (on the mast of a yacht, for example) to get the clearest possible view of the sky. On a handheld unit, however, the antenna is almost always built in.

There are two different kinds of antenna used in handheld receivers: the quadrifilar helix antenna; and the patch, or microstrip antenna. Each has its advantages, but both perform well in most situations.

The quadrifilar helix antenna, like that on the Garmin GPS III Plus receiver, is usually external, and can be swivelled around to improve reception - it functions best when pointing vertically at the sky. It can often be removed from the receiver and placed somewhere else - eg the roof of a vehicle - for better reception.

The patch antenna is much smaller and is almost always inside the receiver – it should be held horizontally, parallel to the sky, for the best reception.

A patch antenna is better at seeing satellites directly overhead, and cannot see ones that lie close to the horizon. A quadrifilar helix antenna is better at seeing satellites low on the horizon, and may be a better choice for travel in remote areas.

CHANNELS

All GPS units manufactured since 1998 have parallel channels, allowing them to track and read data from up to 12 satellites at once. Some older receivers (known as multiplexing receivers) have a single channel, which samples the data from each satellite in turn. These are a little less reliable when moving through dense forest or steep-sided valleys, where trees or terrain may momentarily block the satellite signal.

BATTERIES

Check what kind of batteries your receiver uses and always carry a spare set on day hikes; take a couple of spare sets on multi-day trips. Battery life can range from 12 hours to 30 hours of continuous use depending on the model; this is seriously shortened by prolonged use of the screen backlight.

You can conserve the batteries by switching on the receiver only occasionally to check your position – a set of batteries can last for several weeks. However, if the unit is not on permanently, then some features, such as your speed and direction of travel, will not work.

DISPLAY

The display screen on a handheld GPS receiver is necessarily a small one – around 6 x 4.5cm (2¼ x 1¾in). Handheld displays are usually monochrome LCD screens, with the option of a backlight. However, prolonged use of the backlight tends to burn up the batteries.

The display orientation is usually vertical, but on some models – such as the Garmin GPS III Plus – you can switch between a vertical display for handheld use and a horizontal display for deck or dashboard mounting.

GPS units intended for use in a vehicle or on a boat usually have a larger display so that it can be read comfortably from a distance. Larger and more expensive mapping units may also have a colour screen.

DATA ENTRY KEYS

You input settings and data, and switch between the various screens and functions using a number of data entry keys below (or on certain models above) the display. It is worth trying these out before you buy to see if you can operate the unit comfortably with one hand.

WATER RESISTANCE

Some receivers are advertised as moisture-resistant, some as water-resistant, and others as waterproof. If you are planning to use your GPS in an environment where it may get wet, check out these claims carefully.

Receivers that are not classified as fully waterproof can be protected by buying a special waterproof case manufactured by the company Aquapac International Ltd, 7 Bessemer Park, 250 Milkwood Rd, London SE24 0HG, UK (tel: 020-7738 4466; Internet: www.aquapac.net).

SUN/MOON TIMES

Most GPS receivers contain an almanac that can display sunrise and sunset times, and the phase of the moon, for any given day and position. This can be useful for planning an expedition, or finding out how much daylight you have left when heading back to camp.

COMPUTER INTERFACE

An increasing number of GPS units have the facility to link to a desktop or laptop PC, so that you can transfer data between the two. For example, instead of laboriously measuring the coordinates of a series of waypoints on the map and then manually entering them on your GPS, you can load an electronic map database (provided on CD-ROM) into your PC, and trace out your planned route on the screen using the mouse. A single click will transform the route into a series of waypoints that can then be automatically uploaded to your GPS receiver.

You can also record a route in the field using your GPS receiver, then download the stored route to your PC and show it as an overlay on a digital map. Although some GPS receivers can store and display digital maps themselves, the use of a PC overcomes the problem of limited memory in the receiver.

If you want to use this facility, make sure that your receiver has a data in/data out facility, and conforms to the same transfer protocol as your PC mapping software. The most widely used standards are RTCM 104 for data in, and NMEA 0183 v1.5 and NMEA v2.1 for data out. This information will be supplied in the receiver's technical specifications.

SETTINGS

When you first purchase a GPS receiver, there are several settings that you will have to adjust to suit your intended use.

INITIALIZATION

When the unit is switched on for the first time, or if it has been unused for several months or has been transported more than 500km (300 miles) since it was last used, it will ask you to initialize it. This consists of selecting the nearest city from a list of locations, or manually inputting the approximate coordinates of your position (to within 500km/300miles).

The receiver will then take a few minutes to search for satellites and download almanac data before calculating a position fix. This is known as a cold start. (Remember that you will have to be outdoors so that the receiver has an unobstructed view of the sky.) Once it has worked out where it is, subsequent position fixes will be much faster (warm starts).

MAP DATUM

A map datum (plural data) is a mathematical model of the earth's shape that is used as a reference point for position measurements on maps. There are hundreds of map data in use around the world – make sure that the GPS receiver you use supports the map datum for the map you will be using. You can find a reference to the datum in the map's legend.

Most GPS receivers support the following widely used map data:

● WGS84: World Geodetic System 1984, used worldwide for GPS navigation, and standard on most nautical charts. This is usually the default setting for GPS receivers.
● NAD27: North American Datum 1927, used by most US and Canadian maps published up to the mid-1990s.
● NAD83: North American Datum 1983, used by most US and Canadian maps published after the 1990s.
● GRB36: Ordnance Survey of Great Britain 1936, used on the UK's Ordnance Survey maps.
● AUS84: Australian Geodetic 1984, used on Auslig maps in Australia.

COORDINATE SYSTEM

A coordinate system consists of a grid of intersecting lines that is used to describe a position on a map (see Chapter One). There are several coordinate systems in use, the most common being latitude and longitude, and the Universal Transverse Mercator (UTM) grid. Again, check that your receiver supports the grid system you wish to use.

● Lat/Long: Latitude and longitude, used worldwide on nautical charts, and also usable on most topographic maps
● UTM: Universal Transverse Mercator grid, used on most topographic maps in the USA, Canada, France, Germany and Australia
● OSGB: Ordnance Survey of Great Britain, used on topographic maps in the United Kingdom
● Irish: Irish Grid, used on topographic maps in the Republic of Ireland and Northern Ireland.

NORTH POINT

You can choose whether the bearings displayed by your receiver are calculated with reference to true north or magnetic north. Make sure you know which north point is being used, especially if you are following the bearings using a magnetic compass.

WAYPOINTS

A waypoint, called a landmark by some manufacturers, is a location that is stored in the GPS receiver's memory. It can then be recalled at any time, and the receiver will calculate and display its bearing and distance from your present position.

There are different ways to enter a waypoint. You can read the coordinates from a map, and then manually input them using the data entry keys. Alternatively, you can save your current position as a waypoint so that you can find your way back to it later. If your receiver has a data-in function, you can also upload waypoints from a PC.

Each waypoint you enter is given a unique name (usually no more than six characters). Some units also allow you to assign icons to waypoints to show what they represent (eg a tent symbol for a camp site, a house for a building, or a fish for a good fishing spot).

Check how many waypoints your receiver can store. Figures range from a minimum of 100 to 1000 and more; 500 is average for a handheld unit.

ROUTES

A route is simply a sequence of waypoints joined together in sequence and stored in the GPS receiver's memory. When you select a route, the receiver will lead you to each waypoint in turn; as soon as you reach the first waypoint, it will detect this automatically and change its display to show the direction and distance to the second one, and so on until you reach your destination.

You can enter a route by inputting a list of waypoints manually, or by selecting existing waypoints from the receiver's memory in the desired sequence. You can also use a PC to trace out your desired route on a digital map; the mapping software will then convert this to a list of waypoints that can be uploaded to your receiver.

The route function is particularly useful if your path to your destination follows a twisting course. Check how many routes your receiver can store, and how many waypoints per route (usually up to 50).

TRACK

The track is the actual path that you have followed since starting your journey. Most GPS receivers will store all the fixes obtained since they were switched on, and can plot these on a map screen (see the Navigation screens section below) to show the track you have followed. You can also store a track and download it to a PC later.

GOTO BUTTON

Most receivers have a GOTO (as in 'go to' a location) button. Pressing it brings up a menu of waypoints; you select a waypoint, and the receiver switches to a navigation screen (see next section) showing the distance and direction to the waypoint.

Some receivers have a HOME button. You can specify one particular waypoint as being the home location (eg your camp site). You can then press the HOME button at any time to find the way back 'home'.

PROXIMITY ALARMS

Some receivers offer the option of setting a proximity alarm. This runs in the background and sounds an audible alarm when you come within a specified range of a selected way-point. It can be used to warn you that you are getting too close to a dangerous location, for example shallow rocks at sea, or old mine shafts on land.

NAVIGATING WITH GPS

Using a GPS receiver to navigate is straightforward. It will carry out the basic navigational procedures of fixing your position and measuring the bearing to your destination automatically.

A GPS unit displays its navigational information by means of a range of different 'screens' (referred to as 'pages' by some manufacturers). The actual appearance of the various screens or pages may vary between different manufacturers and models, but the basic principles remain the same.

POSITION SCREEN

The position screen is the most basic function of a GPS receiver. It is simply a numerical readout of your latest position fix, displayed using the coordinate system that you have chosen, along with your elevation, time, and date.

SATELLITE STATUS SCREEN

On some receivers, the satellite status is displayed on the position screen; on others, you have to select a separate satellite status screen from the menu. This screen gives a diagrammatic representation of the relative positions of the satellites that the receiver can see, and which ones it is tracking (ie which ones are being used to calculate the position fix). It also shows the strength of the satellite signal, and an estimate of the accuracy of the position fix.

NAVIGATION SCREENS

Once you have entered the coordinates of one or more waypoints, you can really begin to use the power of GPS navigation. However, note that the graphical displays on the following screens can only be used to full advantage if the receiver is operating continuously while you are moving; they do not function until you begin to move. The unit cannot calculate your speed and direction of travel if you are, of course, standing still.

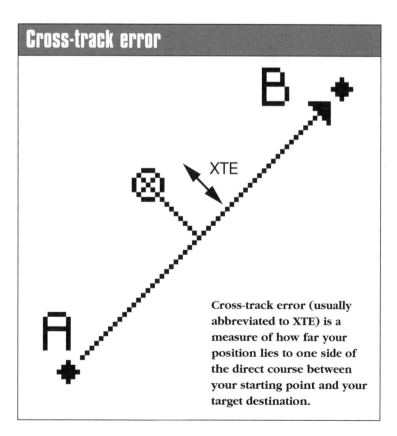

Cross-track error

Cross-track error (usually abbreviated to XTE) is a measure of how far your position lies to one side of the direct course between your starting point and your target destination.

Use the GOTO function, select your target waypoint, and the display will change to a navigation screen. Most receivers will display the three screens described below; you can toggle between them using the arrow keys. If there is no target waypoint selected, the navigation screens will still display your heading and speed, but nothing else.

The receiver updates your position once every second or thereabouts, and uses that information to calculate your heading and speed. These values are also stored as a 'track', a record of your movement over the ground. Most receivers offer a choice of the three navigation screens - the pointer, or compass screen; the highway screen; and the map, or plotter screen.

The illustration below shows these three different screens to illustrate the same situation, where the target waypoint (a small lake, whose position is stored in the receiver's

memory as the waypoint called FISH) lies 0.84km (0.5 mile) away on a bearing of 028°. The user's heading (shown as TRK for track) is 042°, and his speed is 2.3km/h (3.7mph).

The numerical information on a navigation screen includes the name of the target waypoint, the bearing (BRG) and distance (DST) to the waypoint and, if you are moving, the direction you are heading in (HDG or TRK), as well as your speed over the ground (SPD). It may also show the estimated time remaining until you arrive at the waypoint, abbreviated as TTG (Time To Go) or ETE (Estimated Time En route). The graphical display shows your direction of travel (towards the top of the screen), the direction to the next waypoint

Another value that is often displayed on navigation screens is the distance and direction you have strayed from your desired straight-line course. This may be indicated

Navigation screens

A

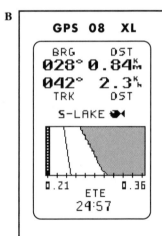

B

C

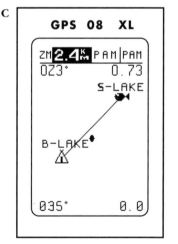

Most GPS receivers offer at least three basic ways for displaying navigational information:

A – The pointer, or compass, screen
B – The highway screen
C – The map, or plotter, screen

graphically by an arrow pointing in the direction you need to turn to get back to the straight-line course (a course deviation indicator, or CDI), or numerically by the cross-track error (XTE), the distance between your current position and the straight-line course.

If you want to save battery power, you can simply make a note of the bearing and distance, switch off the receiver and use your compass to navigate towards the waypoint.

POINTER SCREEN

The pointer screen, also known as the compass screen, shows a graphical representation of the direction to the next waypoint, along with a representation of a compass. This screen is of most use if you are doing most of your navigating with map and compass, and using the GPS occasionally to check the direction to the next waypoint.

In Figure A, the direction of travel is towards the top of the screen, and the direction to the waypoint is shown by a broad arrow – in this case, it is slightly to the left. The points of the compass are shown as they relate to the direction of travel. When the arrow is pointing straight up, you are heading directly towards the waypoint.

Remember that this display is NOT a proper magnetic compass. The north point is only shown relative to the direction of travel. If you stand still and turn in a circle, the arrows will stay fixed. Although it looks like a compass, this screen should be thought of as a diagram.

To use the pointer screen, either read the bearing to the next waypoint and transfer it to your magnetic compass (correcting for declination if necessary), or stand facing your direction of travel with the top of the screen away from you. The broad arrow now points in the direction of the waypoint, and you know that you will have to alter course 14° to the left to head directly towards it.

HIGHWAY SCREEN

This screen is very useful when you are navigating in poor visibility and want to travel in a straight line towards your objective. It shows the direction to your target waypoint in the form of a road or runway extending into the distance, with your direction of travel pointing straight to the top of the screen. As long as the middle of the 'highway' stays in the middle of the screen, you are heading in the right direction.

If you stray to the right of your desired track (as shown in Figure B), the highway will appear to move off to the left of the screen; you must then alter course to the left to bring yourself back on track. As you move towards the waypoint, scale lines on either side of the highway give the impression of moving forward along the imaginary road.

Figure B is just a different way of displaying the same situation as in Figure A. However, the highway screen is easier to follow if you are using the GPS receiver, rather than a magnetic compass, to guide you.

The dotted line along the middle of the highway shows the direction to the waypoint (equivalent to the broad arrow in P). The cross in the centre of the bottom edge of the display shows your position relative to the straight-line course to the waypoint (in this case, to its right).

The figure at the bottom right of the display shows the width of the imaginary highway to either side of the centre line, here set to 0.25km (0.1 mile) – this means that if the position cross on the display moves into the shaded area, you have wandered more than 0.25km (0.1 mile) away from your desired course. The figure at the bottom left of the display shows your cross-track error (XTE), the actual distance you have wandered off course (currently 0.21km).

If you altered your direction of travel to the left and continued travelling, the display would change to show your position gradually moving back to the left until the little cir-

One-handed operation

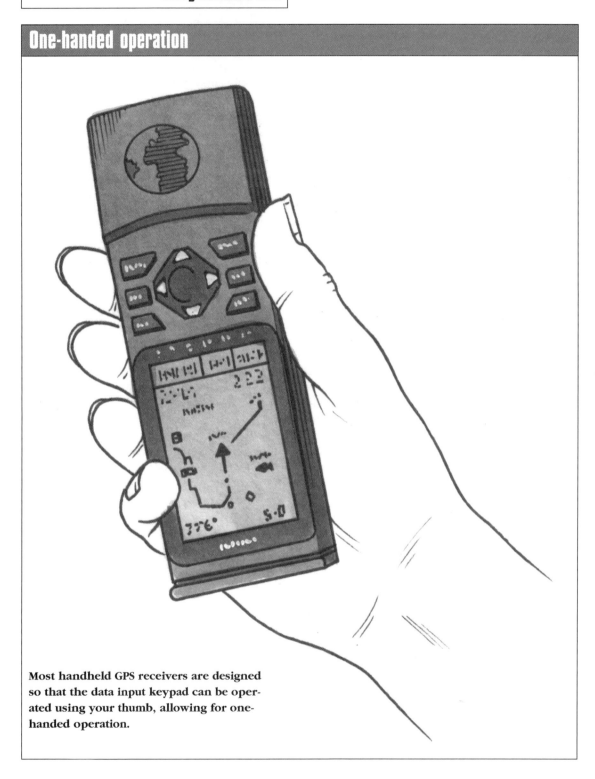

Most handheld GPS receivers are designed so that the data input keypad can be operated using your thumb, allowing for one-handed operation.

cle at the bottom of the screen was in the middle of the highway, and the centre line of the road was aligned with the middle of the top of the screen.

MAP SCREEN

The map screen (Figure C), sometimes called the plotter screen, is a diagrammatic display showing your current position relative to the waypoints stored in the receiver's memory. You can choose to have the top of the screen represent north, your direction of travel, or the direction of the target waypoint. You can choose the scale of the map, and most receivers will also plot your track on the map.

Figure C has north at the top of the screen, and the scale (shown in the bar at the top) set to 2km/1.2 miles (meaning that the width of the screen represents 2km/1.2 miles). The screen shows the same situation as Figures A and B, with the starting point (CAMP), the target waypoint (FISH), the straight-line course between them and the current position (shown by the little cross, northeast of CAMP). Configured in this way, you can easily compare the screen with a paper map.

With the top of the screen set to your direction of travel, your position is shown in the centre of the screen; any waypoints that appear above your position on the display are ahead of you, while any that appear below are behind you.

GPS AT SEA

GPS is particularly useful for navigators in small boats, canoes, and kayaks, because once the receiver is properly set up it can be lashed to a thwart or spray-deck to allow hands-free navigation while you are busy paddling or handling the tiller and mainsheet.

In addition, a GPS receiver will show your heading and speed over the ground rather than through the water. This means that the effect of any tidal streams, currents or wind-related drift will be immediately apparent.

For example, if you are sailing along at 3 knots, but there is a tidal stream of unknown strength flowing against you, a glance at the speed readout on the GPS will reveal your actual speed over the ground. If this reads 2 knots, for example, you will know that the tide is flowing against you at 1 knot.

GPS units designed for use in boats have a special MOB (man overboard) function. When you press the MOB button, the receiver records its current position and switches to a navigation screen that will lead you back to the location where the button was pressed. This can be a lifesaver if someone falls overboard, especially at night. The MOB function is also useful in non-emergency situations, when you want to quickly record the position of a place or object that you want to be able to find again later.

CHAPTER SEVEN

Survival Planning

Survival planning is all about thorough preparation. This applies whether you are the leader of a Himalayan expedition or a parent planning a weekend hiking trip with your family.

People choose to explore the great outdoors for many reasons – enjoyment, exercise, challenge, and adventure. But outdoor pursuits can also be hazardous. Enthusiasm should always be tempered with an appreciation of the possible dangers of your chosen activity, whether it is hiking, climbing, mountain biking, off-piste skiing and snowboarding, sailing, or canoeing.

The best way to avoid potential hazards, and to cope effectively with emergencies when they occur, is to think them through beforehand. Ask yourself the question: "What if?". What if we get trapped by bad weather on the summit? What if I break my leg many miles from base camp? What if the wind strengthens and starts sweeping my boat toward the rocks?

The motto of the Boy Scout movement, 'Be Prepared', says it all. A safe and successful journey requires thorough preparation, good planning, and careful judgement.

● Inform yourself about the area you plan to travel in.
● Make an honest assessment of your physical fitness and abilities, and those of your companions.
● Plan a route that lies within your capabilities, and allow for alternative courses and escape routes.
● Carry suitable safety equipment, and sufficient food and water.

And remember that the preparation does not stop once your trip begins. Keep control of your situation at all times. As you set off each day, think about the terrain you will cover, about possible changes in the weather, and about what you would do if things went wrong. Being prepared is more a state of mind than simply ticking things off on a list.

GETTING INFORMATION

During the planning stages of an expedition, you should obtain as much information as you can about the region you will be travelling in. Order maps and charts of the area, and buy or borrow guidebooks. Find out as much as possible by reading expedition accounts and by talking to people who have visited the area before.

The Internet is a very useful resource for researching an area. Not only can you buy maps and guidebooks online, but many groups and individuals have posted accounts of their expeditions and travels on a web page. Use an Internet search engine such as Google (www.google.com) to search for these types of pages, using the name of the area you plan to visit (along with words such as 'expedition', 'account', 'journal', 'travel diary', and 'journey', as suitable search terms).

ACCESS RESTRICTIONS

Find out about any restrictions there may be on access to the area you intend to travel in. These may apply to privately-owned land, nature reserves that are off-limits to the general public, military firing ranges, hunting reserves, and politically sensitive areas (especially close to international borders). Even national parks, such as Yosemite National Park in the USA, Kakadu National Park in Australia, and Taman Negara in Malaysia, place restrictions on camping and/or hiking in certain areas.

WHEN TO GO

Choosing when to go will be one of your most important planning decisions. The time of year will determine what kind of weather conditions you can expect to encounter, and may mean that certain months will be off-

International map and chart dealers

The following dealers have online shops where you can buy maps and guidebooks from all over the world via the Internet.

Maps.com: 6464 Hollister Ave, Santa Barbara, CA 93117, USA. Tel: 805-685 3100. Internet: www.maps.com

Stanfords: 12–14 Long Acre, London WC2E 9LP, UK. Tel: 020-7836 1321. Internet: www.stanfords.co.uk

World of Maps: 1235 Wellington St, Ottawa, Ontario K1Y 3A3, Canada. Tel: 613-724 6776. Internet: www.worldofmaps.com

World Wide Maps & Guides: 187 George St, Brisbane, Queensland 4001, Australia. Tel: 07-3221 4330. Internet: www.worldwidemaps.com.au

Pre-trip planning

Spend as much time as possible before your trip studying maps, guidebooks and background reading, to familiarize yourself with the area you will be travelling in. Pre-trip planning is an enjoyable pastime, as well as a vital part of your preparations.

itudes the season will affect the amount of daylight, with long days in summer and short days in winter. This effect becomes more extreme the further north or south you go.

There are seasonal hazards to be considered, like hurricanes in the Caribbean and along the eastern seaboard of the USA (June to November), bushfires in Australia and around the Mediterranean (summer); sandstorms in the Sahara desert (summer); and malarial mosquitoes in many tropical and subtropical regions. There are also seasonal irritations, such as the biting insects that plague certain areas in summer (eg blackfly in northern Canada, or midges in the Scottish Highlands).

There are aesthetic factors too. If you plan to visit a popular area like a national park and want to avoid crowds of other people, then avoid high summer and holidays. In temperate latitudes, spring and autumn are often beautiful times of year, with wild flowers blooming in the spring and a blaze of autumn colours in the forest.

limits. For example, desert travel is generally confined to the cooler months, and no one would plan an expedition to Antarctica at any time other than the short southern summer.

The timing of Himalayan expeditions is dominated by the monsoon, which occurs in the northern summer; there are periods of good weather just before and just after the monsoon, in spring and autumn respectively.

SEASONS

The choice of when to go can be influenced by factors other than the weather. In high lat-

WEATHER FORECASTS

As well as reading up on the weather conditions you are likely to encounter, check whether there are any daily weather forecasts that you will also be able to consult.

In national parks and other popular outdoor recreation areas, forecasts are usually posted each day at rangers' huts and information offices. Find out if there are any forecasts on local radio stations; if so, it may be worthwhile for your party to carry a light-weight radio receiver. If you are travelling in a region with mobile phone coverage, check whether there are weather forecasts available by phone; if so, find out the number and carry a mobile (but be aware of how many calls you will be able to make before the battery runs flat).

TRAVELLING AS A GROUP

If you are travelling in a group then your movement should be planned in an organized manner, whether you are a formal expedition or a group of survivors escaping from a crash site. There should be a recognized leader, and everyone should agree to abide by the leader's decisions.

ASSESSMENT

Before you set off, assess your skills and abilities and those of each member of your party. Think about their strengths and weaknesses, and how these might affect your choice of route or objective.

Any adult who has ever been hiking with their children, or has led a school outing, will have experience of making allowances for a group with mixed abilities. It may be less obvious in a group of people who are all of a similar age, but in any such group there will still be those who are strong and confident and those who are less so.

Make sure that the trip you are planning lies within capabilities of the weakest, as well as the least experienced, member of your group. Attempting an objective that lies at the very limit of your ability will leave you with nothing in reserve should an accident occur.

DIVISION OF RESPONSIBILITIES

Group decisions are made more quickly and implemented more effectively if one person is recognized as being overall leader. A good leader will consult all members of the group and listen to their opinions, but his or her decision should be accepted as the final word.

While moving, the leader should be toward the front of the group, and another experienced member should bring up the rear to make sure no stragglers are left behind. If you are heading through difficult or trackless terrain, a good way to make use of fitter and more confident members who may feel frustrated by a slow-moving group is to employ them as scouts, moving ahead of the main body of the expedition to search for the best and easiest route.

In larger groups it is a good idea to adapt the 'buddy system' used by the military by pairing people off. Each member of the group takes responsibility for his or her 'buddy', keeping an eye on them and making sure they are not left behind when the group moves on. If you notice that your buddy is limping, or looking tired, make sure they are OK, and if necessary bring it to the leader's attention. This is a more effective way of keeping tabs on everyone than making the leader responsible for looking after everyone.

RIVER CROSSINGS

Wading across any fast-flowing river or stream that is deeper than knee-height should be avoided if at all possible. If you do have to wade, choose your spot well. In general, on a given stretch of river, the widest places will be the shallowest, while the narrowest spots will the deepest. Try to find a broad, shallow place where you can see the bottom all the way across.

It is best to remove any clothing that is going to get wet. No matter how cold or uncomfortable that may be, it will not be half as miserable as continuing your journey in sopping wet gear. Far better to suffer for a short while and get back into your warm, dry clothes on the far bank.

The only exception to this rule is your

footwear. Do not attempt to wade a river barefoot, unless you can see that the bottom of the river is of smooth sand. Even small rocks can hurt your feet, while wading barefoot on large, slippery stones or boulders is almost certain to knock you off balance. In short, keep your boots on.

If you are carrying a large backpack, leave the waistbelt undone and loosen the shoulder straps a little so that you can easily shrug it off if it threatens to hold you underwater in the event of a slip.

If possible, use a stick or a trekking pole for support. Face upstream, with the pole in front of you to form a tripod, and shuffle across the river bed with small, sideways steps.

USING A SAFETY ROPE

The illustration on page 127 shows the correct way to use a safety rope when crossing a river. One person crosses at a time, and the rope is arranged in a triangle so that the first and last in the water have one rope leading

Travelling as a group

Whether your group consists of mountaineers or family members, assess the strengths and weaknesses of each member **and set objectives that lie within the capabilities of the weakest or least experienced people in the group.**

upstream for support, and one rope to the side, so that they can be hauled back to the bank if they slip. The weakest or least confident members of the party should cross in the middle, with a rope to either bank.

If someone does slip and fall in a fast-flowing stream, haul them in to the bank using the downstream rope. Do NOT keep the upstream rope tight as the pressure of the current can drag them under. If the upstream rope gets jammed in an emergency, be prepared to cut it; keep a knife handy.

PERSONAL PREPARATION

Preparing for your trip involves more than route-planning and sorting out equipment. The physical and mental preparation of each member of the party is just as important for survival in an emergency situation.

Mental preparation involves reading up as much as possible on the geography, terrain and potential hazards of the area you will be visiting, as well as thinking through any emergencies that you might encounter and how you would cope with them.

TRAINING

Physical fitness is important, not only for the day-to-day exertions of hiking, climbing, pedalling, or paddling, but for surviving the extra demands placed on the body by emergency situations. Someone who is physically fit is less prone to casual injuries like sprained ankles, is better able to resist the effects of hypothermia, and has a better chance of escaping from a dangerous situation without need of assistance.

It should be obvious, therefore, that physical training should play a part of your preparation. Unless you are already at a high level of fitness, a thorough training regime should begin at least four months before your trip; train for stamina rather than strength.

Tailor your training to the expected demands of the trip. If your planned expedi-

tion involves carrying a heavy backpack, then include training hikes carrying a similar load.

ACCLIMATIZATION

If you are heading for high mountain areas you should take precautions to avoid altitude sickness, also known as acute mountain sickness, or AMS. The atmospheric pressure of the air we breathe decreases with height. At an altitude of around 5500m (18,000ft) it is 50 per cent of the pressure at sea level. This means that each breath you take at high altitude contains considerably less oxygen than it would at lower altitudes. A rapid change in altitude can bring on AMS, the symptoms of which range from mild to severe, depending on the height, the speed of the ascent, and the person's susceptibility to AMS:

- mild AMS – shortness of breath, mild headache, nausea, fatigue, slight dizziness
- moderate AMS – fatigue, severe headache, persistent nausea, vomiting
- severe AMS – severe fatigue, constant shortness of breath, fluid in the lungs, cyanosis (blue lips and fingernails), cerebral and pulmonary oedema, staggering, confusion, unconsciousness

Fortunately, the body can adapt to reduced oxygen levels, provided that it is given time to acclimatize. The effects of altitude begin to be felt above 2400m (8000ft). Above this height, the body takes around two to three days to acclimatize to the new altitude. So remember to schedule sufficient time for acclimatization when planning a trip to high altitude areas.

The gradual acclimatization provided by hiking in to a high mountain area over a period of several days is much better than the rapid transition created by a helicopter or light aircraft approach.

If any member of your party begins to

Using a rope to cross a river safely

The use of a rope to safeguard a river crossing requires at least three people. One person crosses at a time, while the other two tend the rope. The weakest or least confident members of the group should cross in the middle, with one rope on either side.

the casualty should descend by 300–600m (1000–2000ft) and rest until the symptoms disappear. Severe AMS is a serious, life-threatening condition that requires an immediate, emergency descent of at least 600–1200m (2000–4000ft).

ROUTE PLANNING

The prime consideration when planning a route is not to overestimate the fitness and ability of your party. You may be reasonably fit and have considerable experience of day hikes, but any trip that involves three or more consecutive days of hiking, especially with a full backpack, is a much more difficult proposition.

If you or members of your party have never made a long trip before, it would be wise to begin with a route that has one or more escape options – a cross-country route that links up public transport points would be ideal – so that you could bail out if you get into difficulty.

ROUTE CARDS

A route card can be anything from a page torn out of a notebook to an official, printed document. Its purpose is to provide a written record of your planned route, along with the time you expect to return. A copy of the planned route can then be left behind with a responsible person. If

show symptoms of mild AMS, they should remain at the same altitude and rest for a day or two. For moderate AMS,

you have not contacted this person by the time specified on the card, then he or she will be able to alert the rescue services and give them a clear idea of where to begin searching. On multi-day expeditions, there should be a separate card for each day.

The illustration (right) shows an official route card of the sort used by outdoor sports centres and youth organizations. It includes a table for each leg of the day's route, including its map reference and compass bearing. It may seem overly bureaucratic, but it acts as a useful checklist in planning your trip, and a handy record of your various compass courses – it is easier to measure the various bearings from the map in the comfort of your home or base camp before you set off, rather than in high wind and rain on a mist-shrouded summit. In addition, you can compare your progress with the estimated times on your card, and shorten the trip if you appear to falling behind schedule.

Leaving a route card with someone obviously places a certain responsibility on them; good choices include relatives or close friends, national park rangers, youth hostel or mountain hut wardens and hotel owners. However, you bear an equal responsibility to contact the person concerned as soon as you have safely completed your trip, even if it means going out of your way – or hiking those extra few miles at the end of a long day – to find a telephone.

Route card

ROUTE PLAN

Date: _____ Members of party: _____

Weather forecast: _____

Starting point reference: _____ Description: _____ Time: _____

To (grid reference)	Description (of target)	Direction	Distance	Time (for distance)	Height gain	Time (for height)	Total time	Description (of route and terrain)	Possible alternative route	Escape route

Finishing point reference: _____ Estimated pick-up time: _____

Description: _____ Estimated phone in time: _____

You can buy pre-printed route cards from outdoor equipment suppliers, or design and print your own using the word-processing program on a computer. It does not matter as long as your planner contains the information above.

ESTIMATING TIME

The speed at which you cover the ground will depend on several factors, principally your fitness, experience, the size of the load you are carrying, the terrain, and the weather. Naismith's rule (see boxed text) has proved accurate over many years of use for fit parties on one-day hikes, but if you are carrying a heavy backpack over rough trails your speed will be closer to 3km (2 miles) per hour, falling to 2km (1 ⅓ miles) per hour if any uphill is involved.

A large group will always move considerably more slowly than a small group or a solo traveller. Not only is the group's speed dictated by the slowest member, but there is more hanging around involved, waiting for people to climb over or move around obstacles, or collect their kit together after a meal or rest stop.

ALTERNATIVE ROUTES

You may have noticed that the route card shown here includes space to enter alternative routes. Whether your trip is going to last a day or a week, it is prudent to think of alternative routes on each leg that can be followed in the event of bad weather (eg following a valley or a pass rather than visiting the summit of a mountain, or taking a detour to a bridge rather than fording a stream that is in spate).

ESCAPE ROUTES

There is also a column on the route card for escape routes. These are routes that offer a safe exit from your planned itinerary in the event of an emergency, or a safe route down from high ground if you are caught by bad weather at high altitude. They should be in the form of bearings leading from easily recognizable points along the route.

In mountains, an escape route should begin at a point that you can easily identify in bad weather and poor visibility, and lead down to the safety of a valley as quickly as possible. In remote areas, an escape route should lead to the nearest point where you can contact the rescue services.

The great advantage of planning escape routes in advance is that you have all the necessary bearings and distances written down ready for use, and so do not need to struggle to measure bearings from a wind-blown map. And in the event that a rescue party comes looking for you, they will have an idea of where to look if they realize that you have been overtaken by bad weather.

EQUIPMENT

The amount of equipment that you carry with you will depend on the purpose and duration of your trip. A six-week expedition to the Andes mountains will obviously require more gear than an afternoon's hike in the local state park.

But even on a straightforward walk in an area you know well, your backpack should always contain a few basic safety items, in addition to the usual waterproof jacket,

Naismith's rule

In the late-19th century, the Scottish mountaineer W. Naismith came up with a formula for estimating the time needed for hiking in the Scottish mountains, that still works for many regions today.

The rule states that you allow one hour for every 3 miles (5km), plus an extra 30 minutes for every 1000ft (300m) of ascent. This

assumes a fit and experienced party, and does not include time taken for rest stops, or for coping with difficult terrain and bad weather conditions.

To work out the total ascent, you add together all the uphill sections of the route; no allowance is made for the downhill sections. On a map with a 10m contour

interval (eg the UK's 1:50,000 Landranger series), allow one minute for every contour line.

Thus, if you measure your route on the map and find that it covers 10 miles (16km) and involves a total of 5500ft (1650m) of ascent, your estimate of the hiking time required would be just over six hours (3hr 20min + 2hr 45min = 6hr 5min).

Safety equipment

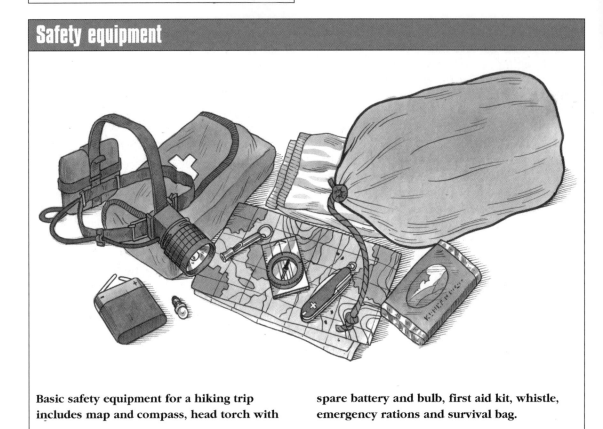

Basic safety equipment for a hiking trip includes map and compass, head torch with **spare battery and bulb, first aid kit, whistle, emergency rations and survival bag.**

spare clothing, and lunch. The minimum safety gear that should be carried on a day hike includes:

- map and compass
- head torch, with spare battery and bulb
- first aid kit
- whistle
- emergency rations (high-energy food)
- survival bag

A survival bag is simply a large – 2.5m by 1.5m (around 8ft by 5ft) – polythene bag, usually coloured orange for visibility, that you can climb inside for protection from the elements. A pocket knife with assorted tools is not absolutely necessary, but is so useful that few experienced hikers or climbers ever

travel without one.

In snow-covered mountains each member of the party should carry an ice axe and crampons, and know how to use them. It is worth adding a bivouac bag and/or light-weight sleeping bag to the emergency clothing in case you have to spend a night in the open. A spare pair of gloves is a good precaution; losing a glove in freezing, windy conditions can be serious.

SAFETY AT SEA

Factors to consider when putting to sea in a small boat include the state of the tide, the location of safe harbour, and the weather, both present and forecast.

Ideal conditions for inexperienced sailors would be a sheltered bay or lake with fine weather and a light breeze of Force 2 to 3. A Force 6 breeze is often described as a 'dinghy sailor's gale' and is the maximum that a small sailing boat can handle safely, even under the control of an experienced helmsman.

In a sea kayak, the only motive power is provided by your own muscles, so it is important to avoid adverse wind conditions. Only strong and experienced paddlers should venture out in winds over Force 3 to 4.

OFFSHORE AND ONSHORE WINDS

When choosing a sailing area, pay special attention to the wind direction as well as strength. A strong offshore wind on an open coast can be dangerous, as you may be blown far out to sea and find yourself unable to get back.

However, a lee shore - where the wind blows towards the coastline - can be just as hazardous in certain conditions. If for any reason (e.g. strong wind, big waves, gear failure) you are unable to make to windward, you could drift downwind onto a rocky shore with breaking waves - a potentially disastrous situation.

SAFETY EQUIPMENT

The safety equipment that should be carried on a small boat, canoe, or kayak includes:

Winter gear

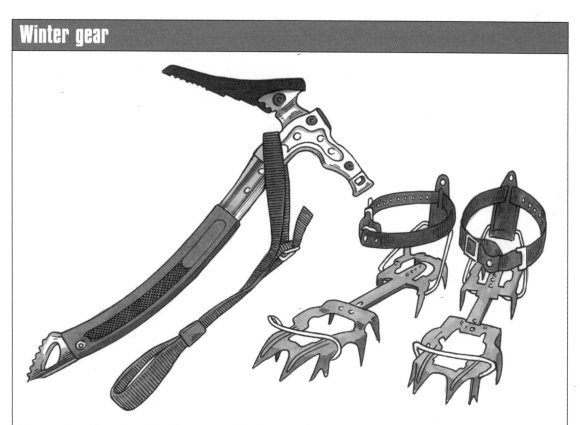

No one should venture into the mountains in winter without carrying an ice axe and crampons and knowing how to use them. One of the main causes of fatal accidents among winter hill-walkers is a slip on snow or ice while not wearing crampons.

The Beaufort Scale

The Beaufort scale of wind force was devised by Rear Admiral Sir Francis Beaufort of the British Royal Navy at the beginning of the 19th century. It describes the force of the wind in relation to its effect rather than its actual speed.

Beaufort Number	Wind speed (knots, km/h, mph)	Description	Effects at sea	Effects on land
0	<1 <1.6 <1	Calm:	Mirror-like calm vertically.	Still; smoke rises
1	1–3 1.6–4.8 1–3	Light Air:	Small, scale-like ripples.	Rising smoke drifts, weather vane is inactive.
2	4–6 6.4–11.3 4–7	Light Breeze:	Small wavelets; crests appear glassy and do not break.	Leaves rustle, can feel wind on your face, weather vane is inactive.
3	7–10 12.9–19.3 8–12	Gentle Breeze:	Large wavelets; crests begin to break.	Leaves and twigs move around. Lightweight flags extend.
4	11–16 20.9–29.0 13–18	Moderate Breeze:	Small waves becoming longer, frequent foamy crests (white horses).	Moves thin branches, raises dust and paper.
5	17–21 30.6–38.6 19–24	Fresh Breeze:	Moderate waves, some spray, many white horses.	Moves large branches, trees sway.
6	22–27 40.2–50.0 25–31	Strong Breeze:	Large waves begin to form; white foam crests everywhere.	Large tree branches move, open wires (such as telephone lines) begin to "whistle", umbrellas are difficult to keep under control.
7	28–33 51.5–61.2 32–38	Near Gale:	Large waves becoming higher; white foam from crests begins to be blown in streaks along the direction of the wind.	Large trees begin to sway, noticeably difficult to walk.

The Beaufort Scale (continued)

8	34–40	62.8–74.0	39–46	Gale:	Moderately high waves of greater length; crests begin to break into spray; foam is blown in well-marked streaks along direction of wind.	Twigs and small branches are broken from trees, walking into the wind is very difficult.
9	41–47	75.6–86.9	47–54	Strong Gale:	High waves; tops of waves begin to topple and roll over; streaks of foam; spray may reduce visibility.	Slight damage occurs to buildings, shingles are blown off roofs.
10	48–55	88.5–101.4	55–63	Storm:	Very high waves with overhanging crests; sea takes on a white appearance as foam is blown in dense streaks; visibility is reduced.	Large trees are uprooted, building damage is considerable.
11	56–63	103.0–115.9	64–72	Violent Storm:	Exceptionally high waves; sea covered with white foam	Extensive widespread damage. These typically occur only at sea, and rarely inland.
12	>63	>115.9	>73	Hurricane:	Air filled with foam; sea completely white with driving spray; visibility greatly reduced.	Extreme destruction.

- chart and compass
- buoyancy aid
- bailer or bilge pump
- spare paddle
- flares
- whistle
- first aid kit
- towing line
- canoe repair kit
- emergency rations
- spare clothing in dry stowage

A sailboat or powerboat should also carry a pair of oars (in case of becalming or engine failure) and an anchor with at least 30m (100ft) of rope.

SURVIVING ACCIDENTS
Most people will never be involved in a serious accident or disaster. However, if you are unlucky enough to be one of the few, you can increase your chances of survival by being aware of a few basic precautions.

TRAFFIC ACCIDENTS
If you are travelling in the less developed parts of the world, cars and buses may not be as well maintained, well equipped, or as safe

The nautical rules of the road

When sailing in busy coastal areas, the hazards of wind and weather are augmented by the risk of collision with other vessels. The International Regulations for the Prevention of Collision at Sea (commonly called the collision regs, colregs, or the rules of the road) is a set of rules that specifies the actions to be taken when there is danger of collision between two vessels.

The rules also specify lights and signals to be used by different kinds of vessels in different situations. Many of the regulations only affect larger boats and ships, but several directly affect small boats, especially those that define right of way.

The more important rules are summarized here. The full text of the regulations can be found in yachting handbooks and on the Internet at www.stormy.ca/marine/colregs.

● Rule 5 – Every vessel shall at all times maintain a proper lookout.

● Rule 8a – Any action taken to avoid collision shall be positive and made in ample time.

● Rule 12a – When two sailing vessels are approaching one another, so as to involve risk of collision, one of them shall keep out of the way of the other as follows:

(i) when each has the wind on a different side, the vessel which has the wind on the port side shall keep out of the way of the other;

(ii) when both have the wind on the same side, the vessel which is to windward shall keep out of the way of the vessel which is to leeward;

(iii) if a vessel with the wind on the port side sees a vessel to windward and cannot determine with certainty whether the other vessel has the wind on the port or on the starboard side, she shall keep out of the way of the other.

● Rule 12b – For the purpose of this Rule the windward side shall be deemed to be the opposite side to that on which the mainsail is carried.

● Rule 13a – Any vessel overtaking any other shall keep out of the way of the vessel being overtaken.

● Rule 14a – When two power-driven vessels are meeting head-on each shall alter her course to starboard so that each shall pass on the port side of the other.

● Rule 15 – When two power driven vessels are crossing so as to involve risk of collision, the vessel which has the other on her own starboard side shall keep out of the way and shall, if circumstances permit, avoid crossing ahead of the other vessel.

as those at home. In addition, the driving abilities of some may be less than we might hope for.

Seat belts in cars are compulsory in many countries, but there are still plenty of places in the world where they are not used, and there are as yet few places where seat belts are fitted on buses. If you are on board a vehicle without seat belts in a situation where you can see that a collision is inevitable, there are certain things you can do to increase your chances of survival.

In a collision, the vehicle will stop suddenly while you are thrown violently forward. As the point of impact approaches, do not put your arms out and brace yourself. Instead, cross your arms in front of your head, turn your head sideways, and throw yourself forward against the dashboard or the seat in front of you, trying to keep your body limp. Easier said than done, certainly, but it works.

PLAN to survive

If you are stranded by an air crash or ship-wreck, use the mnemonic PLAN to remember your priorities:

- Protection – make sure that the survivors are out of immediate danger, and arrange some form of protection from the elements.
- Location – work out your position, contact help if possible, and make signals to attract the attention of rescuers.
- Acquisition – set about acquiring the food, water, and fuel you will need to survive until rescuers arrive
- Navigation – as a last resort, you may have to leave the site of the wreck and make your own way to safety.

AIRCRAFT CRASHES

An aircraft crash is one of the biggest fears of regular air travellers, but in reality a plane crash is a very rare occurrence. Not only that, but statistics show that around 80 per cent of plane crashes are survivable. Certainly there are factors that are outside your control, and some catastrophic crashes will leave no survivors, but there are things you can do to tip the odds in your favour.

- Wear cotton clothing rather than nylon or other synthetics. In the event of a cabin fire it will not melt and is less likely to exacerbate burns.
- Check the location of the nearest emergency exit. Learn how the handle or release operates.
- Count how many rows forward or back it is from your seat to the emergency exit. In a smoke-filled cabin you may have to find it by feel.
- Pay attention to the flight attendant's safety briefing. Learn where your lifejacket is stowed, and how to use it properly.
- Keep your seatbelt fastened snugly at all times.

SURVIVING A CRASH LANDING

Learn the correct brace position – hold your knees and feet together, with your feet slightly forward of your knees; tuck your chin down onto your chest and bend forward, with your hands grabbing your knees or ankles. If you have a cushion or pillow, place it in front of your face.

Rehearse in your mind the sequence of actions you are going to take after the crash landing, so that you can perform them quickly and without panic or confusion. Wait for the aircraft to stop moving; unfasten seatbelt; open the emergency exit, if necessary; leave the aircraft; inflate lifejacket, if necessary. Actually visualize yourself doing these things in the correct order.

If the crash site is on land, get away from the wreck as fast as possible in case of fire or explosion. If the plane has ditched on water, then life rafts will inflate automatically next outside the emergency exits. Never inflate your own life jacket until you are outside the aircraft – it is bulky and can obstruct your exit.

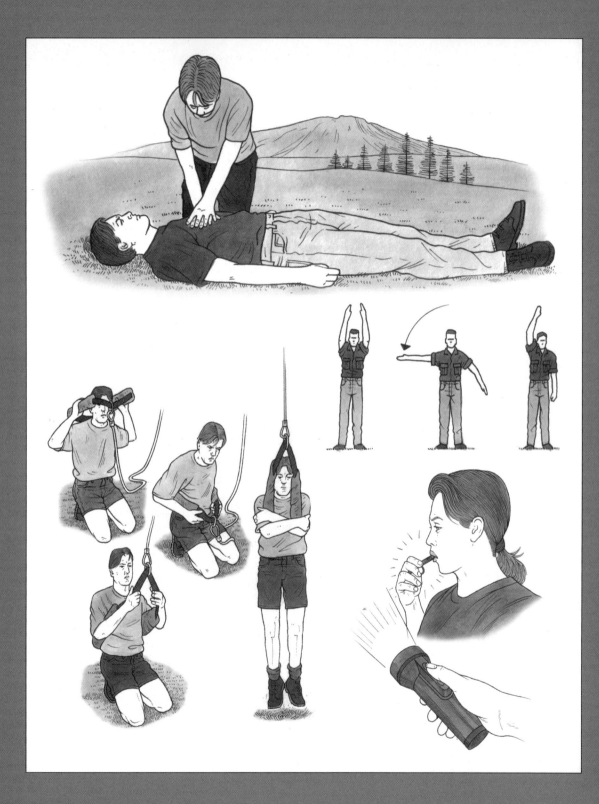

CHAPTER EIGHT

Search and Rescue Procedures

Hopefully you will never need to call out a rescue team. However, in the event of an accident, an understanding of search and rescue procedures will enable you to increase your chances of a safe rescue.

There are two kinds of emergency situation that you might have to deal with if you find yourself stranded in the wilderness – an incident that involves casualties, and one that does not.

In the first instance, your priority will be to administer immediate first aid and enable the casualty (or casualties) to be evacuated to a hospital as soon as possible. This will almost certainly need the help of an outside rescue team.

The second type of emergency usually involves the loss of a vehicle or equipment – such as engine failure in a truck or boat, a forced landing in an aircraft, a dismasted yacht – or being trapped by bad weather or a natural disaster. In this case, lives may not be in immediate danger, but you will need to assess whether you will be able to get out of the predicament without any outside help, or whether you will need to call for assistance.

EMERGENCY PROCEDURE

If your party is unfortunate enough to be involved in an accident, then there is a standard procedure that you should follow.

DO NOT PANIC

The most dangerous part of any emergency situation is the immediate aftermath of the initial accident. The moments of confusion and panic that often occur can result in further accidents and even more casualties.

Try to keep calm and assess the situation before doing anything. The first priority will be to consider – is there still danger present? If someone has just tripped over a rock and broken a leg, it is unlikely that there is any immediate danger to the rest of the party. However, if someone has just been struck by a falling rock, you have to ask yourself where it came from, and why. Is it possible that more rocks might fall? Are you in a gully that is funnelling rockfall from above?

If you decide that the situation remains dangerous, then your first consideration must be to ensure that the casualty – and the rest of your party – are out of danger. There is no point in administering first aid if there is a risk of further injury occurring.

DEALING WITH CASUALTIES

Once you are satisfied that your party is out of immediate danger, your next priority is to deal with any casualties. If more than one person is injured, you will have to prioritize – anyone who is obviously unconscious should be dealt with first, in case they need immediate CPR (which stands for cardio-pulmonary resuscitation); anyone talking, or even screaming in pain, is at least alive and breathing.

The acronym DATE is a useful mnemonic for the four stages required in dealing with each casualty:

● Diagnosis – Evaluate the nature of the patient's illness or injuries

● Assessment – Decide on the most appropriate form of first aid treatment
● Treatment – Deliver and maintain that treatment
● Evacuation – Make arrangements for the casualty to be evacuated to a professional medical centre as quickly as possible.

A full treatment of first aid is beyond the scope of this book, and the following information is given merely as a guide. Anyone planning to travel in remote areas should consider taking a course in first aid, and all parties should at least carry a first aid manual.

Diagnosis

Inspect the casualty all over, checking for obvious wounds and injuries, and palpate the abdomen to check for internal injuries. If the victim is still conscious, ask where the pain is, and whether he or she can move injured limbs.

Assessment

Having decided what is wrong with the patient, you will then have to assess what the treatment should be. This can range from more serious treatment, such as giving CPR, staunching arterial bleeding or splinting broken bones, to less drastic measures, such as cleaning and dressing minor wounds. You will also have to decide whether the group can deal with the situation on its own, or whether you are better advised to call for outside help.

Treatment

Administer suitable treatment. If there is more than one casualty, divide the able-bodied members of the party into teams to deal with the casualties simultaneously.

Evacuation

While treatment is taking place, make plans for evacuating casualties to safety. This will probably involve sending one or more of your party for help.

Sending for help

If you are carrying a radio set, or even a mobile phone, it may be possible to contact the emergency services directly. However, it is more likely that someone will have to hike out to the nearest house or public telephone to summon help.

If there are four or more members in the party, then two people should be sent to get help while the other (or others) remains with the casualty. If there are three of you, then one goes for help and the other stays with the casualty.

If, however, there are only two in the party, then you have a difficult decision to make. In such a situation you will realize the importance of having left details of your planned route with someone back home, or at your departure point (see Chapter Five). If you are in an area where there is the possibility of seeing other hikers, then you should remain with the casualty and try to attract attention. Otherwise, you will have to wait until the person with details of your route raises the alarm. You should only leave a casualty alone as a last resort. Whoever searches for help should take with them the following information, written down clearly in note form:

● The position of the casualty, either as a grid reference or in latitude and longitude. (If you have a spare map, then mark the location of the casualty on it and send it with the messengers)
● A description of the location, eg at 2500m on the west ridge of Mt So-and-so, or five miles upstream of village X on the river Y
● The name and age of the casualty, the nature of his or her injuries, and any first aid treatment that has been given
● The time the accident occurred, and the weather conditions

● The number and condition of the rest of the party
● The equipment available to the party (especially in terms of overnight equipment, such as tents, bivouac bags, etc).

ATTRACTING ATTENTION

Once you have dealt with the immediate aftermath of an accident, you can think about attracting the attention of any rescue party that might be looking for you. This assumes greater importance, of course, if you have not been able to send for help and you are relying on being discovered by a search party.

Fire and smoke

Fire is one of the most useful ways of attracting attention in remote areas. All survival kits should include fire-making materials – waterproof matches, a flint and striker, and a magnifying glass.

Unless you are in an area close to civilization, do not light a signal fire until you are sure that there is someone around to see it. Prepare the fire and keep it covered and dry (with plenty of extra fuel piled nearby) until there is an aircraft in sight, or other evidence of an approaching rescue party.

One fire will usually be sufficient, but three separate fires in the shape of an equilateral triangle is the internationally accepted norm for a distress signal.

By night, a brightly burning fire is what you want, but by day your fire needs to be smoky. You can produce thick white smoke by placing green vegetation on the fire; putting oil or rubber on the fire will produce black smoke. If you have the choice, make smoke that will contrast best with the surrounding terrain (eg black smoke against snow or sand, white smoke against pine forest or dark-coloured earth or rock).

Ground to air signals

The illustration on page 141 shows a set of internationally recognized signals for communicating with a search aircraft. In order to be seen clearly from the air, these signals must be big – at least 10m (33ft) long and 3m (10ft) wide for each 'bar'. You can make them in several ways, but they must be laid out on a flat, open area, in a material or manner that will contrast strongly with their background.

The ideal way is to use the fluorescent orange marker panels that are included in commercial and military survival kits. However, any brightly coloured objects – clothes, waterproof jackets, bivvy bags – can also be used. If nothing seems suitable, pieces of wreckage, stones or tree branches will do.

Other ways of creating these signals include digging trenches in earth, firm sand or snow, and heaping up the spoil on one side in order to create strong shadows.

Body signals

Once an aircraft has spotted you and is flying low to make contact, you can use the standard hand and body signals to communicate with the pilot. If possible, hold a brightly coloured rag or piece of clothing in your hand to emphasize the signals.

Heliograph

Anyone who has travelled by aeroplane and seen the flash of the sun on a window as they approach an airport will know how bright and noticeable such a flash can be. In an emergency, any piece of highly reflective material – a mirror, a piece of glass, polished metal or wreckage, even a compact disc or DVD – can be used to direct the sun's rays toward a rescue party or search aircraft.

To do this, first reflect the sun onto the ground in front of you – you will see it as a small, brightly lit patch. Play around with the reflector until you work out how to move the patch of light in any direction you want. Then, look towards your target and move the reflector so the patch of light moves off in a straight line towards your target.

Another way to do this is to hold the reflector close to your face with one hand while holding your other hand at arm's length so that it lies in front of the target. Then, move the reflector so that the sun's rays fall on your outstretched hand; if you then drop your hand, the beam of reflected sunlight should be aimed towards your target. Wiggle the reflector slightly to create a flashing effect.

A heliograph is simply a hand-sized, rectangular piece of metal polished to a mirror finish on both sides, with a small hole in the centre. It is designed to make aiming the sun's flash at your target much easier and more accurate.

To use a heliograph, hold it just in front of your face and, with one eye closed, sight your target through the hole in the middle. You will see your face reflected in the near side of the heliograph, with a tiny dot of light on it where the sun is shining through the hole. If you now angle the heliograph so that the dot of light on your face appears to disappear into the hole, while keeping the target sighted through the hole, the sun's rays will be reflected directly towards the target.

Flares

All small boats venturing into coastal waters should carry flares for use in an emergency. The minimum number carried should be two orange smokes and two handheld red flares. Parties travelling on land in remote areas might also want to include flares as part of their emergency equipment.

The standard distress signal by day is an orange smoke signal; by night, use a red flare. The red flares can be hand-held (visible up to 8km/5 miles) or parachute flares (visible up to 40km/25 miles). White flares are also available for attracting attention in non-emergency situations; for example, to attract the attention of a large ship at night when there is the danger of collision. (For this reason,

Ground to air signals

A

B

C

D

E

F

G

H

I

J

K

L

M

N

O

P

Q

R

A – Serious injury, need doctor or immediate evacuation
B – Need medical supplies
C – Unable to move on
D – Need food and water
E – Need firearms
F – Need map and compass

G – Need radio or signal lamp
H – Indicate which direction to follow
I – Am moving on in this direction
J – Will attempt to take off
K – Aircraft damaged

L – Safe to land here
M – Need food and oil
N – All is well
O – No, negative
P – Yes, affirmative
Q – Do not understand
R – Need an engineer

Body signals

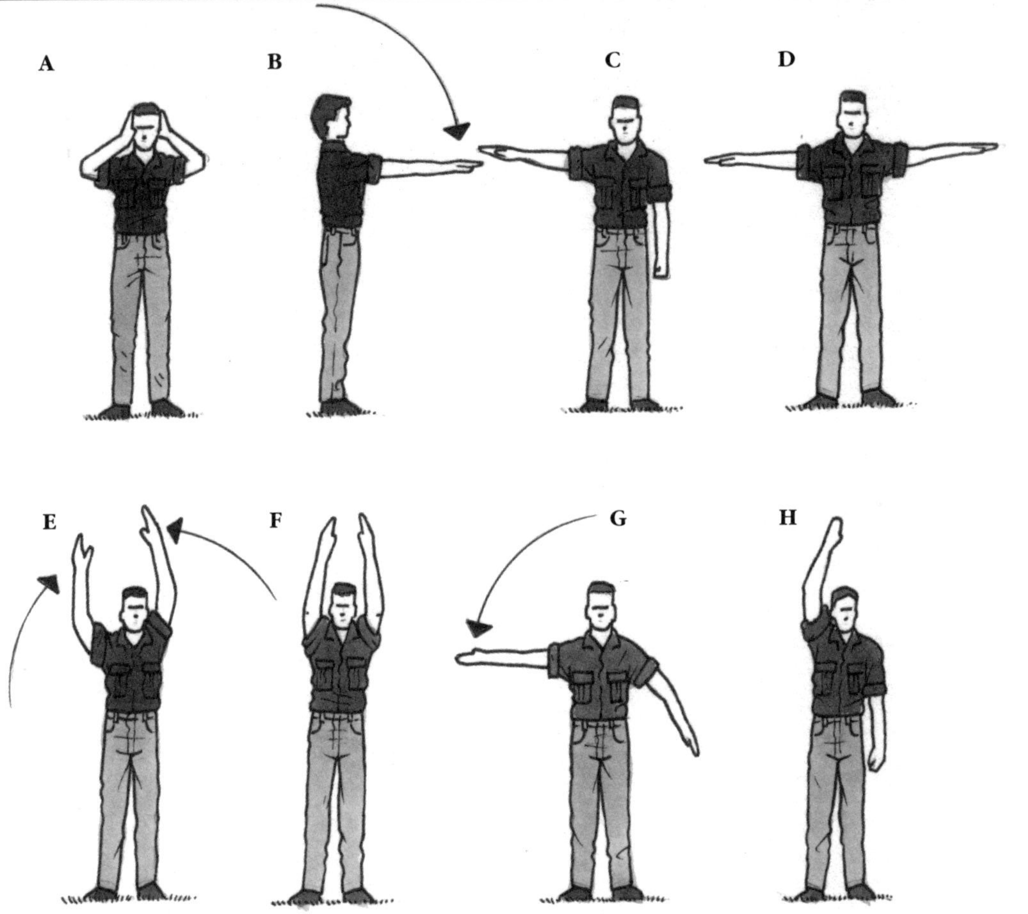

A

B

C

D

E

F

G

H

I

J

A – Our radio is working, communicate by radio

B – Yes, affirmative

C – Can move soon, wait if possible

D – Need engineer, long delay possible

E – Do not land here

F – Safe to land, pick us up

G – Drop a message

H – All is well, do not wait around

I – No, negative

J – Land here

K – Serious injury, need doctor or immediate evacuation

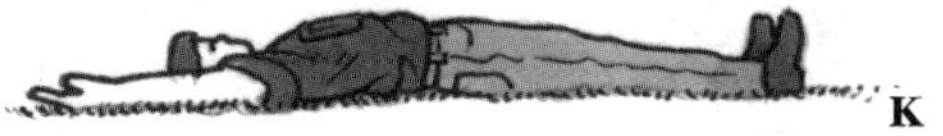

K

white flares are sometimes called 'steamer-scarers'.)

When using a flare, grip the handle at the bottom tightly and point it toward the sky while holding it at arm's length downwind. To ignite it, follow the instructions on the side of the flare. This usually involves twisting a safety lock, and then striking the firing button on the base with the heel of your other hand.

Standard marine flares are relatively bulky and expensive, but it also possible to buy 'mini-flares'. These are sold in a waterproof package containing eight red flares, along with a separate firing handle that is not much larger than a fountain pen. A mini-flare package is easily stowed in a canoe or kayak, and can even be attached to a personal buoyancy aid.

Radio

VHF radios can be very useful in calling for help, but be aware of their limitations. The effective range of a radio depends on several different factors. Most radios can communicate only with other stations that lie in a direct line of sight. In addition, repeated broadcasts of emergency calls at high power will soon drain the batteries.

Most yachts and powerboats carry a marine VHF radio, with the antenna mounted as high as possible, usually at the masthead. The same line-of-sight rule applies, so the range will be further in open water than

International distress signal

The most widely recognized distress signal is six long blasts of a whistle or six flashes of a light in one minute, followed by a minute of silence, and repeated as long as necessary.

among high islands, or along an indented, mountainous coast.

INTERNATIONAL DISTRESS SIGNALS

There are several distress signals that are recognized all over the world.

In the mountains

The international distress signal most widely used in mountain rescue situations is six long blasts of a whistle or six flashes of a light in one minute (ie one blast or flash every 10 seconds), followed a minute of silence, repeated for as long as possible.

The signals can be made in any way possible - six shouts or six waves will do – depending on the situation and the resources available. In quiet conditions with poor visibility (mist or cloud, with little wind) a sound signal will work best. In darkness, torch flashes are more effective. Remember that a rescue team will use the signals to home in on your position, so continue even when you know that help is on the way.

At sea

In the absence of a VHF radio or flares, the following signals can be used to indicate distress at sea:

● The morse code letters SOS - three short, three long and three short signals (. . . _ _ _ . . .), sent by any available means - a flashing torch, a foghorn or other sound
● The boat's ensign hoisted upside down or made fast high in the rigging
● Oily rags burning in a bucket on deck, or any other means of producing smoke
● Rags or clothing tied to an oar and waved aloft
● Slowly and repeatedly raising and lowering your arms outstretched to each side.

HOW A SEARCH PARTY WORKS

If you are in a situation where it is impossible for one of your group to go off in search of assistance, or to call up help by radio or mobile phone, then you will have to rely on being found by a search party.

Provided you have left details of the intended route and timing of your expedition, then the person in possession of these details should alert the rescue services when

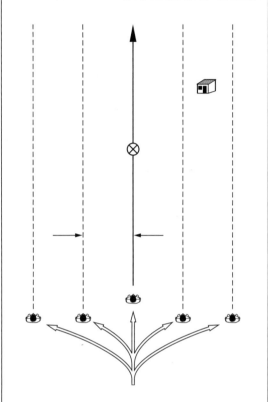

Sweep search

In a sweep search, searchers move in line abreast. The distance between searchers in the line is dictated by the size of the target and the range that can be covered visually by each searcher.

you fail to make any arranged contacts. He or she will thus be able to direct a search party to the correct area.

Search and rescue teams usually consist of professionals or highly trained amateurs. They will use tried and tested techniques that are well adapted to a familiar terrain. Understanding these methods will help you to be aware of how best to attract the attention of a search party.

SEARCH PATTERNS

Any initial search will begin at the last known position of the missing party, and a sweep search will then be focused along their planned route. If this fails to find them, then the search will gradually be expanded to either side of the route. If no planned route is known, then a square search will be used, centred on the last known position.

Sweep search

A sweep search involves a line of searchers spread out across the known route of the lost party, spaced apart at just under twice the distance that can be covered visually by one person. A sweep search can also be used by a party trying to locate a hut, camp or other feature in poor visibility when they are not sure of its exact location. As they approach the area of their objective, they spread out in a line and sweep the area.

Square search

A square search is used to search systematically the area around a last known position when those searching are not sure in which direction their objective lies. It requires a compass and a watch.

Beginning at the last known position, set off in one direction (say south) and walk for a set time (x minutes in the illustration

Square search

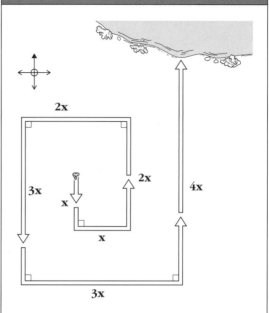

A square search can be used by single searcher. In this case, the search pattern consists of an ever-widening square spiral, working outwards from the estimated or last known position of the target.

above). Turn 90° and walk east for x minutes. Turn 90° again and walk north for 2x

Mayday calls

The standard form for mayday distress calls at sea using VHF radio is as follows:

MAYDAY, MAYDAY, MAYDAY. This is <your vessel's name, three times>. MAYDAY, <your vessel's name once>. My position is <your position>. Briefly state the nature of the emergency, the aid required and the number of people on board. Finish by saying OVER.

Before transmitting, check that the radio is switched on, set to high power and turned to Channel 16. Press the transmit button, pause for a second, and then speak slowly and clearly. Give your position as latitude and longitude, or as a distance and bearing from a known object, eg a lighthouse. Release the transmit button and listen for a reply. If none comes, repeat the message.

minutes, and then west for 2x minutes. Repeat this pattern for as long as necessary. The value of x should be decided by the terrain and the visibility; two is a reasonable figure.

Aircraft search

Aircraft are often used to search large areas. Aircraft searches often take the form of a square search centred on the last known position of the missing party . If you are waiting to be rescued and you see a search aircraft turn through 90°, it does not necessarily mean that the plane has missed you and is heading away. It is probably on a square search pattern and will be back overhead soon – so it's the time to light your signal fires.

HELICOPTER RESCUE

A helicopter is the most widely used method of transport for evacuating casualties from remote areas.

Square search with an aircraft

When there are no factors that would influence the direction in which the target would have drifted (e.g. wind, tide or current), an aircraft search at sea usually takes the form of a square search.

On land

If at all possible, the helicopter pilot will land the aircraft to take on board any casualties. Check out the surrounding area for a potential landing site. It will have to have a clear approach with a fairly level area (slope not greater than 1-in-10), without holes, tree stumps, or other obstructions.

Before the helicopter arrives, remember to weight down any loose items, such as clothing or sleeping bags, in case they are blown away by the down-draught.

At sea

If you are being rescued by helicopter from a yacht at sea, it may be necessary to leave the vessel first because of the danger of the winch line becoming snagged on the mast or rigging. The usual procedure is for the crew to transfer to the yacht's life raft, and for the helicopter's winch-man to be lowered onto that.

USING A HELICOPTER RESCUE STROP

Place the strop over your head and arms, and make it fit snugly under your armpits.

Searching for avalanche victims

When searching for victims buried in an avalanche, speed is important. Statistics show that only 13 per cent of victims buried by an avalanche survive for more than an hour, and only four per cent survive more than three hours.

Using a transceiver

Anyone venturing off piste on skis or on a snowboard should wear an avalanche transceiver and know how to use it. A transceiver is simply a small, combined radio transmitter and receiver that is worn beneath your outer clothing (so that it is not ripped off by the force of an avalanche).

Normally, the device is set to transmit. It is only when someone has been buried by an avalanche that the searchers switch their devices to receive. It is very important that everyone in the party who is safe either switches to receive, or if not actively searching switches off their transceiver.

In the event of an avalanche, begin searching the debris at the point where the victim was last seen. If there are several people with transceivers, spread out in a line across the slope, centred on this point (Fig. 2 – A). If you have to cover a large area of debris on your own, track back and forth across the area, with a gap of about 30m (100ft) between each leg (Fig. 2 – B).

● With your transceiver set to receive, and the volume turned up to full, walk in a straight line downhill. When you pick up a signal (a repeated beep), stop and mark the spot with a backpack, ski pole, or other object (Fig. 1 – A). If several searchers are walking in line, those who have not picked up a signal should stop and switch off their transceiver.

● Continue in a straight line. The signal should increase in strength as you get closer to the victim. Keep on walking until the signal peaks and then begins to fade again. Stop and turn 180° and retrace your steps until you have located the point where the signal is at a maximum. Mark this point (Fig. 1 – B).

● Turn down the volume on your transceiver until you can just hear the signal. Turn 90° to left or right (it makes no difference which) and begin walking again. If the signal begins to fade, turn around 180° and head the other way. (Fig. 1 – C).

● Once you are heading in the direction of an increasing signal, find the next point where the signal peaks and return to it. Mark this spot. (Fig. 1 – D).

● Narrow down the location of the signal even more by holding your transceiver just above the surface of the snow and moving it back and forth in the same, right-angled pattern. The victim's transceiver should now be within a 2m (6ft) square centred on *(contd overleaf)*

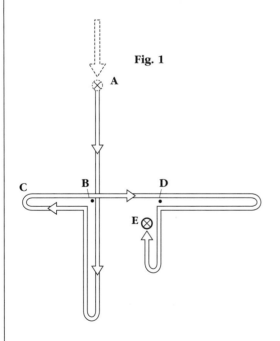

Fig. 1

Searching for avalanche victims (continued)

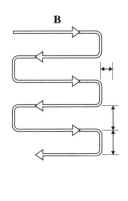

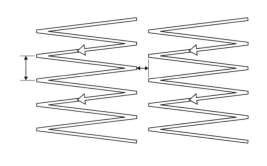

Fig. 2

the spot you have located. (Fig. 1 – E).

● Use an avalanche probe to pinpoint the buried victim, and start digging.

Using a probe

An avalanche probe is a thin metal pole about 3–4m (10–14ft) long. It is made in sections and can be collapsed to 50cm (1.5ft) to fit in a backpack.

The probe is most commonly used to pinpoint the location of a buried avalanche victim after a transceiver search. However, a large rescue team equipped with probes can also search avalanche debris using probes alone, if the victim was not wearing a transceiver.

The standard search pattern involves a line of rescuers spaced 0.75m (2.5ft) apart. Each person probes the spot between their feet, takes one pace forward, probes again, and so on (Fig. 3).

This method is very time consuming and labour intensive, and is only used as a last resort after a visual search of the surface and a search using sniffer dogs has been unsuccessful.

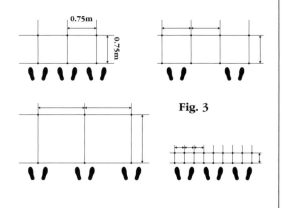

Fig. 3

Tighten the strop by sliding the adjusting ring down towards your chest. When you are ready to be lifted, give a thumbs up to the winch-man. Keep your arms folded across your chest, or held down vertically at your sides. Never hold onto the strop above your head, or you will risk sliding out of it.

BASIC FIRST AID

There are a few basic first aid procedures that anyone venturing into remote areas should be familiar with, whether trained first aiders or not.

HYPOTHERMIA

Hypothermia is a condition in which the body's core temperature falls to a dangerously

Helicopter rescue strop

During a helicopter rescue, you will probably be winched into the aircraft using a rescue strop. Place the strop under your armpits, tighten up the adjusting ring, and keep your arms folded (or held straight down at your sides) while being lifted.

may seem innocuous, but they can progress rapidly to a dangerous level.

● In the early stages of hypothermia, the victim complains of feeling cold and suffers from bouts of intense shivering. The victim's attention may wander, and he may have difficulty using his fingers (to tie laces or fasten and unfasten zips, for example).

● In the middle stages, as the victim's core temperature falls below 33° C (90° F), shivering stops as the body begins trying to preserve energy and shuts down the blood supply to the extremities. Once the shivering stops, the situation has become serious.

● The victim feels weak, disoriented and unwilling to do anything, and his skin looks pale. He may appear confused, even drunk, with slurred speech and staggering gait. He may experience double vision. His skin – even on the abdomen under his clothing – will feel cold to the touch. He will probably have an overwhelming desire to go to sleep.

● If left untreated at this stage, unconsciousness and death will follow.

Treatment
Treatment of hypothermia consists of a gradual rewarming of the patient. In cases of mild hypothermia, this can usually be done without calling for outside help.

low level, generally defined as below 35° C (95° F). It is caused by continuous exposure to cold, wet and windy weather, or by immersion in cold water.

Symptoms
There are several stages of hypothermia, ranging from mild to severe. The initial symptoms

● Get the casualty into a sheltered place, out of the wind and rain. Pitch a tent or dig a snow cave if necessary.

● Wrap the casualty in a blanket or, better still, a sleeping bag. Make sure his head is covered – the head is the main area of heat loss. Be sure to place insulation between the victim and the ground as well.

● Apply gentle rewarming. The best way to do this is for one or more healthy members of the party to get into the sleeping bag alongside the victim. If a bath and hot water are available, immerse the victim in warm (not hot) water (38–40° C, or 100.4–104° F).

● If the victim is conscious, encourage him to drink warm, sweet drinks (sugary tea is good) and nibble some glucose tablets.

There are certain things you should never do with hypothermia victims. Never put them into a hot bath (over 40° C, or 104° F). Never give them alcoholic drinks. Never rub their hands or feet to warm them up. All of these actions can result in a rush of blood to the already cold extremities, which can cause a potentially fatal further cooling of the body's core.

Do not remove wet clothing either, as the resulting evaporation of moisture on the victim's body can also cause further cooling.

Severe hypothermia should be treated in the same way as mild hypothermia, but evacuation to a hospital as quickly as possible is essential. The rewarming process can be assisted by applying thermal packs (chemical hand-warmers, bottles of warm water or stones heated in a fire and wrapped in clothing) to parts of the body where core blood vessels lie close to the skin – between the thighs, the back of the neck, small of the back and the pit of the stomach. Do not apply heat to the extremities.

A victim of severe hypothermia will be unconscious and pale, with low respiration and a weak pulse. He may appear dead, but do not give up rewarming and resuscitation until you are 100 per cent certain that the victim is beyond recovery; hypothermia victims with core temperatures as low as 30° C (86° F) have been resuscitated successfully.

HEAT EXHAUSTION AND HEATSTROKE

Heat exhaustion is caused by severe dehydration resulting from prolonged exertion in hot conditions. It is easily prevented by ensuring that you drink enough fluids.

Heatstroke (or hyperthermia) is the advanced stage of heat exhaustion, and can be very dangerous. The body's normal temperature regulation system breaks down and the core temperature rises to 40° C (104° F) and above.

Symptoms

● The initial signs of heat exhaustion include general fatigue, increased pulse and respiration rates, pale complexion and feelings of weakness and dizziness.

● Continued exertion will lead to muscle cramps, nausea and vomiting, caused by dehydration and loss of salt through sweating.

● If the condition advances into heatstroke, the victim will become delirious and eventually fall into unconsciousness and coma.

Treatment

Treatment for heat exhaustion consists of cooling and rehydrating the victim.

● Move the casualty to a cool and shady spot. Help her to lie down, with her feet raised (propped on a backpack, for example). Splash the casualty with water and then fan her, or expose her to any breeze to assist cooling.

● Administer a rehydration drink (see boxed text, Rehydration drink), getting the victim to take small but frequent sips rather than gulping down a large quantity at once.

● The casualty should continue to rest and drink until her urine output returns to normal. This can take several hours and several litres of drinking water.

Rehydration drink

You can make up a rehydration drink to treat a victim of heat exhaustion by dissolving one level teaspoon of salt and eight teaspoons of sugar in a litre of water.

Alternatively, salt may be added in similar proportions to fruit juice or a commercial fizzy drink (make sure it contains sugar, and is not a diet drink). If sugar is not available, then just add salt.

● If heatstroke is suspected, cool the victim by wrapping her in wet sheets or wet clothing. Keep dampening the sheets or clothes as necessary.

FRACTURES

Diagnosing a broken bone is usually fairly straightforward. However, if you are in any doubt as to whether you are dealing with a break or a sprain, treat the injury as if it is a fracture.

Symptoms

● An open fracture, where the broken end of the bone is protruding through the skin, is obvious.
● A closed fracture may be indicated by a deformity of the limb (compare the injured limb with the healthy one), or by bruising, swelling, and tenderness.
● If the victim cannot move the limb, or put weight on it, a fracture is likely.

Treatment

Your priority in an emergency situation will be to immobilize the fractured limb until the casualty can be evacuated.

● An effective splint should immobilize the joints on either side of the broken bone. A splint for a broken forearm, for example,

should immobilize both the elbow and wrist joints.
● Objects that can be used for makeshift leg splints include an ice axe, ski pole or trekking pole.
● A wrist fracture can be immobilized by wrapping some stiff material around the hand and forearm – a newspaper, magazine or even a folded map – and tying it with a bootlace or piece of cord.
● When binding a splint, be sure not to restrict the circulation.
● If necessary, further stabilize the fracture by binding the splinted limb to an uninjured part of the body. For example, a splinted leg can be bound to the other leg.

CPR

CPR stands for cardio-pulmonary resuscitation, a technique that combines artificial respiration (mouth-to-mouth ventilation) of the casualty's lungs with cardiac massage (rhythmic chest compression) to pump oxygenated blood around the body.

It is used when the casualty has stopped breathing and has no pulse (ie the heart has stopped beating). As such, it is a technique of last resort. You should seek training in CPR, and practise the method before you actually need it. The situations in which you might need to use CPR include drowning, severe hypothermia and heart attack.

● If the victim is not breathing, check that the airway is clear (use a finger to remove any blockages in the mouth, eg vomit or dentures). Tilt the victim's head back to open the airway, placing one hand on the forehead and using the other to lift the point of the chin.
● Pinch the victim's nostrils closed, and place your mouth over the victim's mouth to form a seal. Breathe out to inflate the victim's lungs, then remove your mouth to let the air out, watching the victim's chest to make sure it rises and falls. Give six quick inflations to

CPR

Cardio-pulmonary resuscitation (CPR) is the combination of mouth-to-mouth artificial respiration (to deliver oxygen to the victim's blood stream) and cardiac massage (to pump the oxygenated blood around the body. Knowledge of CPR is a vital first aid skill.

begin with, followed by one breath every five seconds.

● After the first six inflations, check for a pulse. If there is a pulse, then continue with the artificial respiration. If there is no pulse, begin cardiac massage.

● Kneel beside or astride the casualty, and locate the breastbone by running a finger up the edge of the ribcage; place the heel of one hand about two fingers' width above the lower edge of the breastbone.

● Place the heel of your other hand on top of the first, lean over the casualty and with straight arms press the breastbone down by 4–5cm (1.5–2in). Repeat at the rate of three beats every two seconds.

● Alternate six beats of cardiac massage with one inflation of the lungs. Do not try to give both at the same time. This is easier if there are two first aiders, one working on the heart, the other on the lungs.

● If you have to give CPR alone (and this is very hard work), alternate 15 beats of cardiac massage to two inflations to reduce the amount of position-shifting required.

● Frequently check for a pulse. Do not continue cardiac massage if the victim's heart has started beating.

THE RECOVERY POSITION

Any casualty who is unconscious or semi-conscious should be placed in the recovery position, unless serious injuries – to the head or spine, for example – prevent it. Lay the casualty face down, with the arm and leg on one side placed at right angles to the body, and with the knee and elbow bent. Turn the head to the same side, and rest the face on the hand (see illustration opposite).

This position allows for easy breathing, and any fluid or vomit can drain freely from the mouth instead of blocking the airway.

The recovery position

Unconscious accident victims should be placed in the recovery position to ease breathing and minimize the risk of choking on vomit. Make sure the victim is warm and comfortable.

First aid kit

The following checklist should be regarded as the minimum contents of a first aid kit for wilderness travel. The items should be packed in a strong, waterproof container, clearly marked with the words 'First Aid'.

● Surgical gloves for the first aider (to protect against blood-transmitted diseases, such as AIDS or hepatitis)
● Plastic airway
● Assorted wound dressings
● Burn dressing
● Adhesive dressings for small cuts and grazes
● Zinc oxide adhesive tape
● Crepe bandage

● Antiseptic wipes
● Antiseptic cream
● Sterile needle
● Safety pins
● Thermometer
● Diarrhoea medication
● Painkillers (paracetamol and ibuprofen)
● Salt tablets
● Antihistamine pills and cream (for insect bites and stings)
● Special dressing for foot blisters (e.g. Second Skin or Compeed)
● First aid instruction leaflet
● Paper and pencil (to note down information to pass on to the rescue team).

CHAPTER NINE

Tracking and Trailing

The art of the navigator lies in conducting a journey safely, using map, compass and observation. The art of the tracker lies in reconstructing a journey made by a human or an animal, using observation of the marks and signs left behind along that journey's route.

Tracking is one of the oldest skills possessed by the human race. To primitive hunters, good tracking often meant the difference between life and death, between a successful hunt and starvation. These ancient skills and secrets still survive, handed down from generation to generation, among native peoples scattered around the world, notably the Aborigines of Australia, the forest tribes of Africa, Borneo, Indonesia and South America, and the native Americans of the USA and Canada.

In recent years there has been a great resurgence of interest in tracking as more and more people have taken up outdoor pursuits. But where tracking skills were once used to put food on the table, they are now used to gain a deeper insight into nature. They are also used to get close to animals that would otherwise never be seen, either for the purpose of taking wildlife photographs, or just for the challenge and the simple pleasure of observation.

Tracking human beings is almost as old a skill as hunting animals, but has been perfected more recently by military special forces units around the world. This chapter will also look at the techniques used by military trackers.

OBSERVATION

Successful tracking depends on meticulous observation. In their daily lives, most city people do not tend to observe what goes on around them. On the contrary, they often try to shut the rest of the world out, concentrating on work, conversation, TV, a book or a magazine. Many carry over this attitude when they go hiking for recreation, hurrying along a trail, chatting to their friends, checking their watches to see if they will make camp by dinner time.

If you want to become a tracker, you will need to escape from this mindset, to slow down and open yourself up to the slower rhythms of the natural world. You need to develop the ability to look at things without expectation or the need to know the name of every flower, bird or butterfly you see. More important is seeing animals and birds behaving naturally, unaware of your presence. This kind of observation is a skill that can be learned, and improved, through practice.

OBSERVING BIRDS AND ANIMALS

The best way to learn about the habits and movements of birds and animals is to watch them. You will have to spend a long time – several hours at least – sitting quietly and unobtrusively, just watching and waiting. Your aim should be to see more than just the animals themselves; you want to see and understand their patterns of behaviour.

Here are some guidelines for increasing your chances of spotting wildlife:

- Stay quiet
- Get off the beaten track
- Choose your spot carefully
- Look low down, and look for small animals
- Have patience.

Staying quiet does not just mean not talking. It means moving quietly, which is a difficult thing to do in thick brush. Animals have acute hearing and the merest snap of a twig will see them moving off long before you even have a chance of catching sight of them.

The reason that most people do not see too much wildlife when they are out hiking is that most people stick to a trail. Animals are not stupid. They know that hiking trails are regularly used by humans, and they stay well away from them. If you want to spot wildlife, you will have to get off the beaten track and out into some real wilderness.

The best places to look for animals are areas featuring plenty of food, water and cover for them to hide in. The edge of a forest where trees give way to undergrowth, or a tall-grass meadow beside a lake or river are ideal spots. Lush vegetation and trees in fruit attract small animals and larger herbivores, which in turn attract predators such as hawks, foxes, and wildcats.

Wildlife programmes on television and photographs in books and magazines have given many of us an exaggerated idea of the size of many animals. When you finally see them in real life, most creatures are actually much smaller than you might expect. They also spend most of their time in cover, surrounded by bushes and undergrowth. So sit down, stay low and look into rather than over the undergrowth.

The most important quality in watching wildlife is patience. There is no substitute for finding a good hide or vantage point and just waiting. More than likely, in time, the animal you are waiting for will come along.

LOOKING FOR MOVEMENT

The human eye is very good at picking up

movement. Try this experiment. While looking straight ahead, hold one hand straight out to your side; you should still be able to see it out of the corner of your eye. Keep your eyes forward, but move your hand backward until it is just out of sight. Now wiggle your fingers. Although you may not be able to see the actual fingers of your hand, you can still detect their movement, even at the very edge of your visual field.

The best way to look for movement is not to scan the landscape continuously , but to choose some point in the distance and gaze steadily towards it. Do not focus your attention on this spot, but try to become aware of your entire field of vision without moving your eyes around. In this way any sudden movement will immediately draw your attention to that spot.

The movement of vegetation is often the first sign of an approaching animal, so watch for the twitching or swaying of grass, bushes, undergrowth or tree branches, and then concentrate on that area.

LOOKING IN CLOSE-UP

The world of small mammals, such as weasels, field mice and voles, exists down on the ground, way below a human's normal field of vision. You can learn a lot about nature by studying a small patch of ground – a square metre, or yard, for example – in great detail. Get down on your hands and knees and get your head right down next to the ground. Look for the little runs and trails in the grass made by these small animals, and for the sign they have left behind – tiny footprints, droppings or tufts of fur.

STAYING HIDDEN

Whether you are watching wildlife or tracking an enemy patrol, staying hidden is a vital skill. To avoid being seen, you need to understand what kinds of things attract attention in the first place.

THINGS THAT ATTRACT ATTENTION

The human eye is attuned to picking out certain types of features:

● Shape - distinctive shapes, especially the outline of the human body
● Silhouettes - anything silhouetted against the skyline
● Regular spacing – any objects or marks that are spaced in a regular pattern
● Shadows - the contrast of a shadow, especially a moving shadow, on a sunlit surface
● Shine - anything that reflects sunlight
● Contrast - any surface that contrasts with its surroundings, eg a pale face against dark foliage
● Movement - anything that moves against its background.

These are the sort of areas that an observer should be alert to. They are also important

The ghillie suit

The ghillie suit – named for the Scottish ghillies, or gamekeepers, who first used the concept in the 19th century – is the preferred camouflage of military snipers. A ghillie suit is simply an outer coverall or jacket of coarse camouflage netting, to which strips of coarse hessian have been tied. In the field, pieces of natural vegetation are added to the suit.

The effect is to create three-dimensional 'noise' which conceals the sniper's outline. The hessian strips and pieces of vegetation produce genuine dark shadows – a natural shadow is around two orders of magnitude darker than the darkest black fabric.

A cover made with the same technique can be used to conceal a rifle or a telephoto lens.

Things that attract attention

A – The human outline
B – Moving shadows
C – Silhouette
D – A flash of reflected
   sunlight
E – Contrast (pale face on
   dark vegetation)
F – Movement
G – Regular spaced people or objects

factors to consider for anyone trying to remain hidden.

CAMOUFLAGE AND CONCEALMENT

Camouflage, in the context of tracking, is defined as the exploitation of natural surroundings or artificial aids in order to conceal, or disguise, your presence.

Your aim when stalking is to blend into the background, so consider the factors that tend to attract attention, and think about how to minimize them while you are moving.

The first area to think about is clothing. Choose drab, neutral colours, but make each item of clothing – trousers, shirt or jacket, headgear – a different shade; if they are all the same, they are more likely to reveal your outline. Tailor the colours to match the environment in which you will be operating. If you have pale skin, use charcoal, dirt or face paint to darken your face and hands.

The patterns on military camouflage clothing are designed to break up the outline of the wearer, but each is designed for a particular environment, be it jungle, desert or arctic. Do not think that any green camouflage clothing will work in any forest, or that the desert camouflage used in the Gulf War will work in the Australian desert, for example.

As well as colour, think about your shape. Assume a position that makes your body blend in with the natural shapes and forms around you. In a forest, stand straight with your arms by your sides, like a tree trunk; on open moorland with scattered boulders, stay crouched with your knees drawn up. If you have climbed a tree, lay along a branch rather than sitting up on it. In woodland or open country that lacks natural cover, military snipers and some wildlife photographers wear a ghillie suit that uses colour, shape and texture to create a camouflage effect.

SHINE AND LIGHT

Conceal or cover any piece of kit which has a smooth or polished surface which might reflect a flash of sunlight, including wristwatch, eyeglasses, binoculars or map cases. This applies at night too, as moonlight can be reflected in the same way. In the dark, do not use flashlights or cigarettes.

SILHOUETTE AND SHADOW

Always be aware of what is behind you (from the point of view of your quarry). Try to place yourself in front of a backdrop that will help to hide you, and never allow yourself to be caught on the skyline.

Use shadows for hiding in, and do not allow your own shadow to be cast in such a way that it signals your presence. In the illustration (Figure B), the man on the left is using shadow to conceal himself; the shadow of the man on the right announces his arrival ahead of him.

WIND

When tracking animals, always stay downwind so that the breeze does not carry your scent to them. This is easier said than done; wind direction is rarely constant, especially in the turbulence around trees and hillsides, and it is difficult to keep track of what it is doing at all times. Prey animals such as deer and antelope can detect human scent on the wind at a distance of about 1000m (3000ft).

OTHER ANIMALS

When you are tracking an animal, do not forget that there are lots of other animals and birds nearby, and frightening any of these could well alert your quarry to your presence. Many birds and animals have an alarm call which can be heard at a great distance – disturb one of them and the wildlife for hundreds of metres around will know you are there.

This also applies when stalking humans, but in this case an animal's alarm calls can work in your favour, alerting you to the presence of your quarry.

Blending in

Try to blend in with your environment. Adopt a pose that mimics the shape of the natural features around you: stand upright among forest tree trunks; lay flat along a horizontal branch; sit down among boulders on a hillside.

KNOW YOUR QUARRY

If you want to get really close to an animal quarry, you need intimate knowledge of its habits and behaviour. You can learn a lot from books, videos and TV, but you can only obtain true knowledge through experience. When tracking an animal, you need to know what it feeds on, where it feeds, where it goes for water and what trails it follows.

When tracking a human you have the advantage of being able to make informed guesses as to what your quarry's movements and motivations might be, but the rule still applies. The more you know about him or her, the better you will be able to track them successfully.

SIGN

When people think of tracking, they immediately think of following a set of footprints. But a footprint is only one example of sign. Sign is any physical indication left by the passage of an animal, human or vehicle through the environment. Most sign used by human trackers is visual, but there are examples of olfactory sign (eg horse manure, bear musk, camp fire smoke) and audible sign (bird and animal calls, human voices, breaking twigs, rustling vegetation). Visual sign is usually divided into ground sign and top sign.

Ground sign

Ground sign is anything that lies below ankle height, and is mostly caused by the action of the quarry's feet. As animals and people move through the environment, they not only leave footprints (where the ground is soft enough), but also leave behind droppings or litter, knock small stones out of place, break twigs and make marks on vegetation.

Examples of ground sign include:

- Footprints
- Scuff marks made by feet
- Bruised or marked grass or leaves

- Broken twigs that have been stepped on
- Disturbed leaves, twigs or stones
- Animal droppings
- Fur or feathers
- Animal burrows, nests and scrapes
- Litter, cigarette ends, chewing gum
- An old camp fire
- Grass flattened by a tent at a camp site

Top sign

Top sign lies above ankle height, and consists mainly of disturbances in vegetation caused by the passage of the quarry's body, head and upper limbs.

Examples of top sign include:

- Grass swept forward by leg movement
- Broken grass stems, briars, twigs and branches
- Fur or feathers caught on twigs or thorns
- Broken spider webs
- Disturbed dew on vegetation
- Trodden-down fences
- Blazes cut into tree bark
- Machete marks on vegetation
- Clothing threads caught on thorns or twigs.

TRACKS

A track is basically a line of footprints, or more correctly a line of sign. This section is concerned with general features that apply to all kinds of tracks.

TRACK CHARACTERISTICS

Each individual, whether animal or human, leaves behind a unique set of tracks, and close study of them can reveal a great deal about your quarry. If they belong to an animal, they can tell you its species, size, how it was moving and what it was feeding on. If they belong to a human, you can learn their size and type of footwear, their height and weight, whether they were walking or running, and whether they were injured or were carrying a load of some sort.

When you first come across a track, there are many features that you need to examine. It is best if you jot these down in a notebook. The most important features are the shape and size of the footprints, stride length, register and gait.

MEASURING TRACKS

Taking note of the basic features of a track allows you to confirm that you are still following the same quarry should you lose the trail for a while and then pick it up again.

Make a sketch of the shape and appearance of one of the prints. Then measure the various features listed below and record your findings in a notebook. The following features can be measured for almost any set of tracks:

- Length (A) and width (B) of the individual footprints
- Length of stride (C), measured from heel to heel, or toe to toe
- Straddle (D), measured between the inside edges of the prints, or from outside edge to outside edge
- Pitch (E), the angle between the long axis of a footprint and the direction of travel.

REGISTER

Register is a feature of a four-legged animal's track. It refers to where the print of the hind foot lies in relation to the forefoot print (on the same side).

Watch a domestic cat walking, for example, and you will see that it places its hind foot in almost exactly the same place that its forefoot has just been lifted from. This is called direct register, and the track left by a cat shows the hind paw-print directly on top the corresponding fore paw-print.

Different animals have different register when walking. A bear's hind paw is almost always behind its front paw, while a hare's hind footprint is almost always in front of its fore footprint.

Measuring tracks

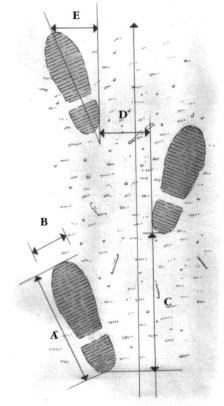

Measurable track characteristics include:
A – Length
B – Width
C – Stride length
D – Straddle
E – Pitch

In addition, the same animal may show different register depending on how it is moving. For example, a running cat places its hind paws on the ground well in front of its fore paws.

Register can sometimes be used to identify an individual animal. Native American trackers could tell different horses apart by noting the position of front and rear hoof prints in relation to each other.

GAIT

Gait refers to an animal's style of walking or running, ie how it moves its legs. There are five basic animal gaits that you should be able to recognize.

Diagonal walk

Animals whose legs are all the same length - horses, deer, cats and dogs, for example - move their feet in a diagonal pattern when walking. The order in which their feet touch the ground will be something like: front right, hind left, front left, hind right. Their tracks show close or direct register, with the hind foot stepping close to, or directly on, the print of the front foot on the same side.

Pace

Animals such as bears, beavers, raccoons, badgers, wombats and camels move the limbs on one side of their bodies at the same time, shuffling along as they move their weight from side to side. Their stepping order is front right, hind right, front left, hind left. This means that the hind foot always registers behind the forefoot.

Bound

Animals with legs that are short in relation to the length of their body - such as stoats, weasels, mink, martens - move along with a bounding motion, bringing their hind feet up close behind their forefeet before reaching forward with the forefeet again. This gait produces a track with all four footprints clustered close together, the hind prints behind or beside the fore prints, with large gaps between each cluster of prints.

Gallop

Animals whose hind legs are much longer than their forelegs - such as rabbits, hares, squirrels, gerbils, wallabies and kangaroos - walk with a sort of slow, leapfrogging gait, planting their forefeet in front of them and then bringing their long rear legs forward on either side, so that the hind feet hit the ground ahead of the forefeet.

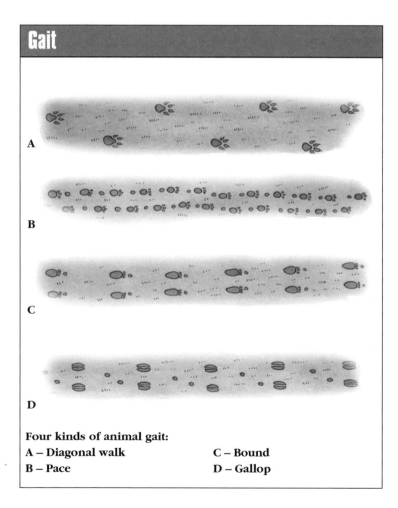

Gait

Four kinds of animal gait:

A – Diagonal walk	C – Bound
B – Pace	D – Gallop

Most diagonal walkers also develop a galloping gait when they are running rather than walking. When a cheetah, which can reach speeds of up to 110km/hr (70mph), is sprinting in pursuit of its prey, its hind paws can hit the ground a couple of metres in front of its rear paws.

Hop

Hopping is a two-legged gait, and is therefore confined to birds and a few animals with long hind limbs, such as kangaroos, wallabies and gerbils when they are moving quickly. The resulting track is easily imagined, with two hind prints side by side, and no fore prints.

DISTINGUISHING MARKS

Footprints, whether animal or human, may also have distinguishing marks or characteristics that allow you to identify a particular individual among groups of similar prints. For example, an animal may have suffered some injury to its foot that has left a scar that shows up on a pad print, or a nick in its hoof that shows in the outline of the print.

In humans, the pattern of wear on the soles of their shoes are often distinctive. Depending on the way they walk, their soles may wear faster on the outside or inside of the foot, or at the heel or toe. When tracking, look out for and make a note of any such distinguishing marks.

BASIC TRACKING SKILLS

The goal of a tracker is to locate, interpret and follow sign. The skills needed in order to do this quickly and efficiently take many years of practice and experience to develop.

PURSUING A TRACK

When you come across a track, there is a set

Making a tracking stick

A tracking stick is a useful tool, and very simple to make. Take a fairly straight length of stick and place one end at the back edge of the print you are tracking. Mark the front edge of print on the stick (cut a notch, or slide a rubber band along the stick) to show the length of the print. Then mark the back edge of the next print to show the stride length.

Whenever the trail becomes unclear, you can use the stick to show where the next print should lie.

procedure you should follow – do not just blunder off in the general direction of the trail.
● Consider the environment or habitat in which you found the sign
● Identify and measure the first sign
● Assess the direction of travel
● Look for the next sign.

ENVIRONMENT

Before you begin to make a close examination of the track, first consider the environment or habitat in which it lies, and ask yourself the following questions:

● What kind of vegetation is there?
● How much food and cover is there?
● What kind of animals would you expect in an area like this?
● Where is the nearest water source?
● What was your quarry doing here?
● Was it passing through on the way to somewhere else, or was it feeding, sleeping or hunting?
● What is the weather like, and what has it been like? How will this affect the track?

IDENTIFICATION AND MEASUREMENT

Once you have pondered these questions, you can set about identifying and measuring the track, taking note of gait, register, and any distinguishing marks. Think about what kind of animal it is – male, female, large, small, old or young. Try to judge the age of the track.

TRACKS

Close examination of the track should tell you your quarry's general direction of travel. Stand up and look in this direction; try to deduce where your quarry is heading. Is it heading into the forest or going down to the river to drink? Is it taking food back to its burrow to feed its young?

FINDING THE NEXT SIGN

Use your measurements of print size and stride length to look for the next sign. This task is made a lot easier if you use a tracking stick (see boxed text, Making a tracking stick). As you follow the track, do not step on the footprints; keep to one side. Right-handed trackers usually walk to the left of the track they are following.

As you pursue the track, try to find every single footprint. This will provide you with a lot of information as to how your quarry was moving, as well as in which direction it was moving. This knowledge can provide valuable clues as to where it might be heading, and how likely you are to catch up with it.

Move forward as stealthily as you can, checking ahead frequently to see if your quarry is within sight. Make frequent 'SLLS' halts – stop, look, listen, smell. Once you have made visual contact with the quarry, you can switch from track pursuit to stalking techniques.

LOOKING FOR SIGN

When you are examining sign, get your head down close beside the ground. Low-angled sunlight, towards the beginning and end of the day, shining across your direction vision, is best for highlighting tracks.

SIDEHEADING

To see really faint tracks on firmer surfaces, use the technique called 'sideheading'. Lay one side of your head flat on the ground and look horizontally along the surface, keeping the tracks between you and the light source. (This technique also works well for finding small objects you have dropped on the floor at home; a pin or tiny grub screw may not be obvious from above, but using sideheading, you can find it easily.)

SCANNING

When you are looking for the next sign, systematically scan the area in front of you with your eyes, covering a semicircle of around 5m (17ft) diameter.

Military track pursuit drill

Trackers in special forces units are trained to follow a rigid track pursuit drill when tracking a potentially hostile human quarry. The drill consists of seven steps, all of which are undertaken while staying hidden and moving with stealth:

● Assess the quarry's general direction of travel.
● If there is more than one choice of route ahead, examine them and eliminate all except the one with the quarry's track.
● Look ahead for the furthest sign on the track, and connect it back to the first sign.
● Check ahead to see if the quarry is in sight.
● Check to left and right of the track to see if deception tactics have been used.
● Work out the best route to the furthest sign.
● Move forward with stealth, and repeat the drill until you have the quarry within sight.

DIRECTION OF TRAVEL

Although a good set of tracks clearly indicates the quarry's direction of travel, there will be places where the tracks become less distinct. However, there are other signs that show which way your quarry is headed.

In areas of vegetation, look for branches or twigs broken or bent forward, or grass trodden down in the direction of travel. Any fur, hair or clothing threads caught on thorns or barbed wire will be hooked or draped over the rear edge of the obstruction. Broken spider webs are good direction indicators as they stick to the vegetation ahead of them as the quarry brushes past.

On firm or stony ground, look for stones that have been nudged or kicked out of position. You may be able to spot a slightly darker patch of damp soil at the stone's original position, or even a small hole or depression where the stone once lay. The direction in which it was kicked gives an indication of direction of travel.

DISPLACEMENT

Displacement of sign occurs when the movement of the quarry has transferred one substance (eg water or soil) onto another surface (eg rock or vegetation). This happens when the quarry moves from one kind of terrain to another.

Examples include water transferred onto the rocks of a riverbank as the quarry climbs out of the water; mud transferred from a patch of muddy ground to the stalks and leaves of grass and vegetation on the far side; and wet sand carried on the quarry's feet from a sandy bank into the dry grass above it.

Displacement can also take the form of foliage, moss, twigs or stones that have been scuffed, kicked or snagged out of their original position.

THINGS THAT AFFECT SIGN

The quality of sign is dependent on many factors, including the terrain, the past and present weather conditions, the presence of other animals and humans, and the age of the sign.

Terrain

The nature of the terrain will have a large influence on the type and quality of sign. Open forests with plenty of undergrowth make ideal tracking territory, as it is almost impossible for an animal or human to move through such country without leaving plenty of evidence of its passage.

Grassland, moorland and open farmland is more of a challenge, especially when there is a lack of cover, but there is still plenty of scope for finding sign. Tracks in grass show up as areas of different shine or colour where the grass blades have been flattened; a track through wet grass is even easier to follow.

Rocky ground or hard, dry earth is difficult tracking terrain, but far from impossible. Here you will have to concentrate on looking for very shallow impressions on dusty surfaces, scuff marks, displaced stones and twigs, and stone fragments pressed into the earth. A tracking stick is a great help in such conditions.

Dry, sandy desert poses the most difficult tracking challenge. Dry sand does not take a sharp imprint, and a wind can obliterate tracks within minutes.

Firm, wet sand, on the other hand, as found on a seashore or riverbank, is one of the easiest tracking mediums. This surface preserves prints very clearly, but there is always the danger of a rising tide or river level washing the track away.

Weather

Heavy rain can wash away all tracks, while a prolonged spell of hot, sunny weather can leave the ground dry, hard and unreceptive to imprints. A light shower, on the other hand, can prove useful in timing a track; if there are raindrop marks on the footprint, your quarry must have passed before the

Direction of travel

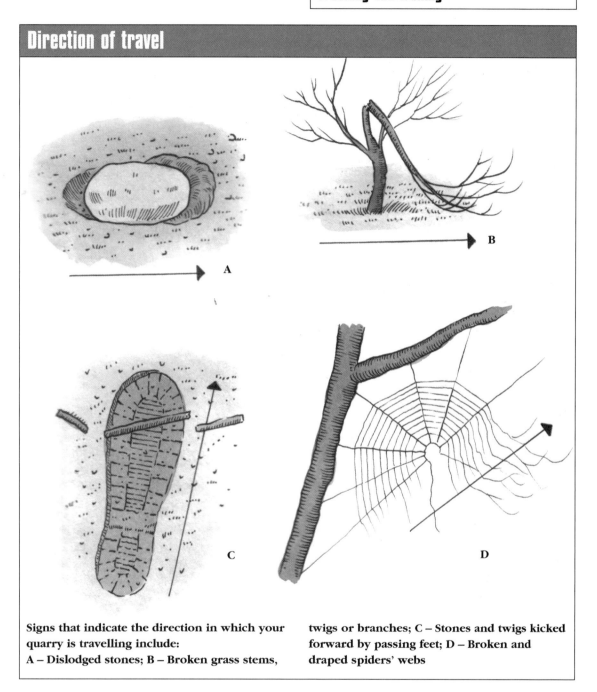

Signs that indicate the direction in which your quarry is travelling include:
A – Dislodged stones; B – Broken grass stems, twigs or branches; C – Stones and twigs kicked forward by passing feet; D – Broken and draped spiders' webs

rain fell. Record the times of any such showers in your notebook, in case they prove useful in this regard.

Strong winds can disrupt top sign in vegetation and blow dust, leaves and debris onto tracks. Heavy snowfall will conceal everything,

Displacement of sign

 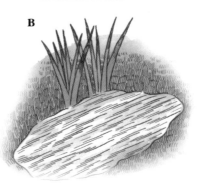 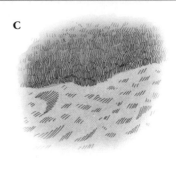

When the quarry moves from one type of surface to another, it leaves displaced sign:
A – Water on rocks
B – Mud on vegetation
C – Sand on grass

but leave a perfect surface for tracking once the flakes have stopped falling.

Third-party sign

The movements of other animals and humans in your area can foul the track of your quarry and make it more difficult to follow. If there are only a few other animals, you should be able to pick out your quarry's sign with a bit of effort. However, if a whole flock of sheep has crossed your trail it may be impossible to continue.

JUDGING THE AGE OF SIGN

Judging how much time has passed since your quarry left its track is an art in itself, and one of the most difficult aspects of tracking. The three factors mentioned above – terrain, weather, and third-party sign – all contribute to the way sign deteriorates over time, and to how easy or difficult it will be to judge its age.

Estimating the age of sign accurately is important in distinguishing old from fresh sign and in judging how far behind your quarry you are. The latter can be a matter of life and death if you are tracking a human enemy.

There is no way that a book can tell you how old a track is. This is a skill that can be learned only by long experience, helped by making your own aging experiments (see boxed text, Aging experiments, on opposite page).

Among the many things to think about are the nature of the ground (hard or soft) and its aspect (is it sheltered or exposed to rain and/or sun?); the weather (has it rained recently?); and the activity of other wildlife, humans and vehicles in the area (will they have superimposed their tracks on those of your quarry?).

You can gain some insight, especially when tracking human quarry, by making your own fresh footprint alongside the sign you are tracking and comparing the two, or by snapping a fresh twig and comparing its colour and appearance with a twig broken by your quarry.

STALKING

In recent years the word 'stalking' has taken on a rather sinister meaning, usually that of the persistent following or harassment of another person. It is used here, however, in its traditional sense, that of following or getting close to your quarry by moving quietly and stealthily.

Like tracking, stalking is an ancient skill, originally used by hunters to get close enough to their prey to make a kill. It is still used in this sense in the sport of deer-stalking.

The art of moving silently and stealthily through forest and brush is not easy to learn. It requires much practice and no small amount of fitness. To move slowly and smoothly, without sudden movement or loss of balance, needs as much strength and muscle control as a gymnast or ballet dancer.

STEALTH

Stealth is defined as the act of moving with extreme care and quietness in order to avoid detection. Stealthy movement requires care and thought to make the best use of cover, and silence to avoid alerting the quarry. The best approach to your quarry is rarely direct – choose the route that offers the best cover, while remaining downwind (if your quarry is an animal).

Even when walking normally, you should always take care to move silently. Do not tread on dry leaves, twigs or rotten wood, and do not step in soft mud that may make a sucking noise as you lift your foot.

Try to go around rather than through thick undergrowth, but if you do have to pass between bushes, do not just squeeze through and let the branches spring back. Gently lift the vegetation with your hand, move past it and carefully lower it again. And never grab hold of a branch or sapling for support when climbing or descending a slope, or when getting up from a crouch or crawl; this practice is known to soldiers as flag-waving (see boxed text).

THE STALKING CROUCH

The final approach to your quarry requires even more caution and concentration than usual. The stalking crouch is a posture and way of moving silently that must have been developed by hunters thousands of years ago, and is still used by native trackers and hunters today.

Bend your legs slightly, and place your hands on your thighs just above the knee.

Aging experiments

You can learn a lot about how sign ages by carrying out your own aging experiments. Ideally, this should be carried in the area in which you intend tracking, but you can do it in your own garden or backyard.

Mark off an area of soil about a metre or yard square, and make a few of your own footprints in it. If possible, get your pet dog or cat to add some of theirs too. In addition, place one or two freshly broken twigs, some leaves, and some litter (a candy wrapper or cigarette end).

Note the time and then return to examine your plot after one hour, six hours, 12 hours, a day, two days, a week – whenever you can, taking note of both the weather conditions and the ways in which the various 'signs' change over time.

You can extend such experiments to include fresh animal droppings, discarded food, camp fires and any other variety of sign you can think of.

Move slowly and carefully forward by high-stepping – lifting your foot high, above knee height, and keeping the toes pointed forward and down so they do not catch on any twigs or vegetation. While balancing on one leg, place your foot slowly and gently down, feeling with your toes for any dry leaves or twigs. If necessary, push these gently aside or move your foot to another spot. Once you have found a safe spot, touch down the outside edge of your foot first, then roll it onto the ball of your foot, before finally bringing your heel slowly down and slowly shifting your weight onto it. Then repeat this slow, high-stepping movement.

Try to move as smoothly as possible. The first time you attempt this, you will realize how difficult and tiring it is to stand on one foot on uneven ground while trying not to wobble or lose your balance. It requires a great deal of strength in the muscles of the foot and leg. Practice is of course essential.

Keep your eyes on the quarry at all times, and synchronize your movements with its

Stalking

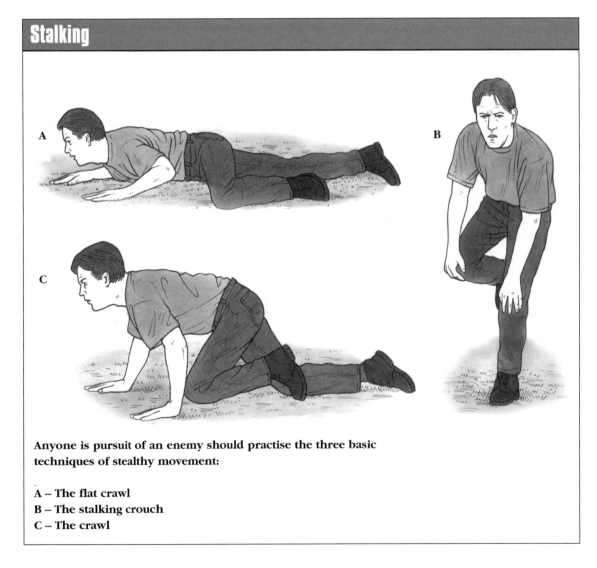

Anyone is pursuit of an enemy should practise the three basic techniques of stealthy movement:

A – The flat crawl
B – The stalking crouch
C – The crawl

own. Move while it is feeding or looking elsewhere, and freeze whenever it turns its head in your direction.

THE CRAWL

Where cover is scarce and low, or when you are getting really close to your quarry, you will need to drop into a crawl. The principles of movement are the same as for the stalking crouch –

slow, deliberate, and silent. Keep your body low, and try to avoid sticking your backside in the air; your head should be the highest part of your body, but still kept low.

Imitate the movements of a stalking cat. Feel ahead with one hand at a time, compressing the ground gently before putting your weight on it and, as you move forward, bring your knee up to occupy the spot just vacated by your hand. Do not drag your foot along the ground; raise your knee and ankle by the same amount, with your toes pointed backward, so that your lower leg moves parallel to the ground and your foot does not catch on anything.

THE FLAT CRAWL

For the final approach to your quarry, you may need to adopt a flat crawl. To shift from a crawl to a flat crawl, keep edging forward with your hands while your knees stay in the same place, and slowly ease your belly down onto the ground as gently as possible.

Keep your toes turned out of the way so that your heels do not stick up. Move forward by taking your weight on your forearms, feet and lower legs, and inching along a little at a time. Moving in this way is extremely tiring, especially on the abdominal muscles. Beginners will find it hard to move more than a metre or two.

If there is enough cover to raise your body a little, you can roll slightly to one side and bring your upper leg forward until the knee is at right angles to your body, and take your weight on that as you move forward.

To get up from a flat crawl, slowly reverse the process of dropping onto your belly, pushing back with your hands until you are back in the crawl position.

FREEZING

If at any time you think your quarry has spotted you, freeze. Stop in the middle of whatever you are doing and stand absolutely still, even if you are standing on one leg in the middle of taking a step. If your quarry does not immediately bolt, there is a good chance that it has not seen you, and if you have taken care to blend in with your background, it probably will not. Wait until it looks away or returns to feeding before moving silently towards cover, freezing again if necessary, should it look towards you again.

Your natural instinct in such a situation may be to jump back or drop down into cover, but any sudden movement will see your quarry disappearing quickly over the horizon. Develop the self-control and muscle strength necessary to freeze and hold your posture stock still.

TRACKING ANIMALS

There are many reasons for tracking animals, from hunting to wildlife photography, or conservation. Many amateur trackers do it for fun, and to increase their understanding of the natural world.

IDENTIFYING ANIMAL TRACKS

Recognizing individual species of animals by their footprints is just one facet of the tracker's art, but an important and enjoyable one. It can take many years to become proficient in this, but you should be able to learn how to identify the major species of animals with just a little practice. To learn more, go to a bookstore and buy a field guide to animal tracks.

There are several families of animal whose members all leave similar footprints, and whose tracks distinguish them from other families.

The single-hoofed family

Horses and their relations (eg zebras) have single, rounded hooves. A horse that has been shod has a very distinctive print that most people are familiar with.

The cloven-hoofed family

Cloven-hoofed animals include cattle, sheep, goats, pigs, wild boar, deer, elk and moose. Prints left by these animals show two solid toes split by a single cleft.

The bear family

Bear tracks are large and have five toes on both front and back feet, usually with claw marks showing. The rear prints are quite long and sometimes look a little like a barefoot human print.

The dog family

Dogs, foxes, wolves, and coyotes have a central, roughly triangular or heart-shaped pad with four toes on each foot, front and back, and usually with claw marks.

The cat family

Like dogs, members of the cat family (including the domestic cat, wildcat, lynx, lion, and tiger) have a central pad and four toes on each foot, but the prints are usually more rounded than those of the dog family, and do not show claw marks.

The rabbit family

Rabbits and hares have soft, rounded central pads with four toes, though sometimes the toes do not show separately; their claws are not usually seen in the prints. The hind feet are much larger than the fore feet.

The rodent family

Rodents include rats, mice, voles, squirrels, chipmunks and beavers. Rodent prints vary greatly in size from species to species, but all have five toes on the rear feet and only four on the front, usually with claws showing.

ANIMAL SIGNS

In addition to their tracks, there are many other kinds of sign that animals leave behind. These can range from gnawed acorns (squirrel) to mud wallows (rhinoceros). The most common marks are scratches left by claws on earth and tree bark; rubs caused by an animal squeezing under, over or between branches, or by deer rubbing their antlers on a tree trunk or fence post; gnaw marks left by rodents on twigs and pieces of bone, or more obviously, by beavers on tree stumps and branches; and tufts of hair or fur left behind on twigs, thorns and barbed wire.

Droppings

The faeces, or droppings (known as 'scat' in North America), left behind by animals can provide clues as to the species and diet of your quarry. Droppings are also a good time indicator.

Trails and runs

Most animals are creatures of habit, and their daily comings and goings between sleeping place, feeding place and watering place leave

Tracking kit

Take the following kit with you when you go tracking:

- Field guide
- Map and compass
- Notebook and pencil
- Tape measure (3m/10ft)
- Ruler (15cm/6in)
- Magnifying glass.

trails and runs through the vegetation that can be seen and followed by the tracker.

TRACKING HUMANS

Tracking other humans is usually associated with spies, snipers, secret agents and special forces soldiers. But there are more peaceful uses for this aspect of the tracker's art, notably that of finding people who have become lost while hiking in the mountains or forest.

The fundamental skills of tracking humans are identical to those for tracking animals. The big difference is that the tracker will have a much better insight into the psychology and possible motivations of his quarry. In general, humans are much easier for a beginner to follow, because they tend to leave a lot of obvious sign, and even a beginner can make educated guesses about where his or her quarry is likely to be heading and what sort of things they might do along the way.

You can make a quick estimate of how many people are in a group by counting the number of footprints in a 1m (3ft) long section of track and dividing the total by two. Speed of movement can be guessed by looking at length of stride (long = fast) and whether the heel marks are deeper than the toe marks.

IDENTIFYING INDIVIDUALS

You can identify an individual person by examining and measuring their tracks closely, and noting the size, type (and possibly manufacturer) of their footwear, and recording any distinctive pattern of wear on the soles. A measurement of stride length will give an idea of their height, and the depth of the footprint will provide an indication of weight (compare both with your own).

Finally, look for a distinctive gait. Does your quarry walk with one or both feet pointed slightly inwards, outwards or straight ahead? Is there any asymmetry in the prints? A deeper imprint on one foot might indicate a limp, for example, or someone carrying a heavy shoulder bag.

JUDGING MOVEMENT FROM FOOTPRINTS

Examination of footprints can tell you whether a person was walking slowly, walking quickly, jogging or running flat out. First of all, think about how your own footprint is made when you are walking at an average pace on level ground (see the illustration on page 174). If you like, go and find a stretch of soft ground and walk or

Track report

When military trackers come across a possible enemy trail, the first thing they do is to make out a track report containing the following information:

- Tread pattern, depth, gait (make of footwear?)
- Direction of travel (compass bearing)
- Number of persons
- Speed of movement (estimate)
- Load (are the tracks deeper than expected?)
- Age (how fresh are the tracks).

Human footprints

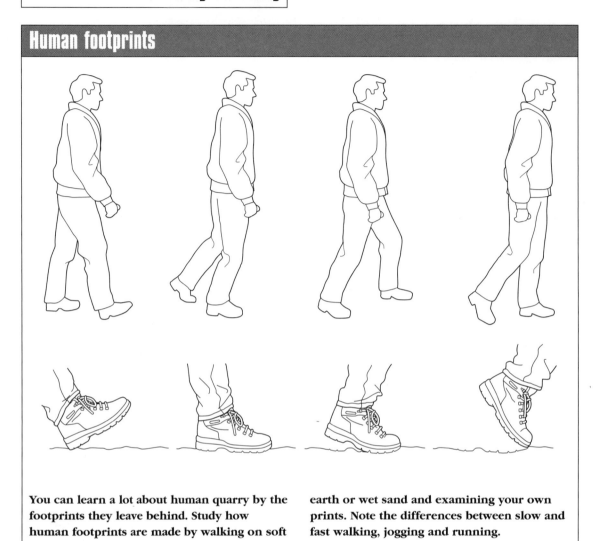

You can learn a lot about human quarry by the footprints they leave behind. Study how human footprints are made by walking on soft earth or wet sand and examining your own prints. Note the differences between slow and fast walking, jogging and running.

run across it at various speeds, and then note the differences in your tracks.

The first part of your foot to hit the ground is your heel (A), which digs in, compressing the soil downwards and forwards. As you move forward and place your weight on your foot, the sole levels out and makes a complete print (B). Then, as your other leg comes forward, your heel raises sharply (C), before you finally push off on the ball of your foot and your toes (D). As your foot moves forward, the toe may drag lightly along the ground.

WALKING SLOWLY

When you walk slowly, you tend to place your feet further apart than usual, your toes point out a little more and your heel does not hit the ground with such force at A.

WALKING QUICKLY

When you walk quickly, your stride length

increases slightly, your toes point further forwards and you push off from the ball of your foot with greater force at C and D. This makes the footprint a bit deeper at the front, with a slight heaping of earth behind the toe in soft ground.

JOGGING

When jogging, your stride length increases again and your straddle decreases (ie your left and right footprints lie closer to the centre line of your track). The imprint of your heels will be lighter, and those of your toes deeper.

RUNNING

If you are running flat out, your footprints will lie along an almost straight line and your stride length will be at a maximum. The prints will have almost no heel marks, but the toe marks will be deep with a pronounced 'push-back'. As your foot comes forward out of the print it will leave a plume of dirt forward of the toe.

Hand signals

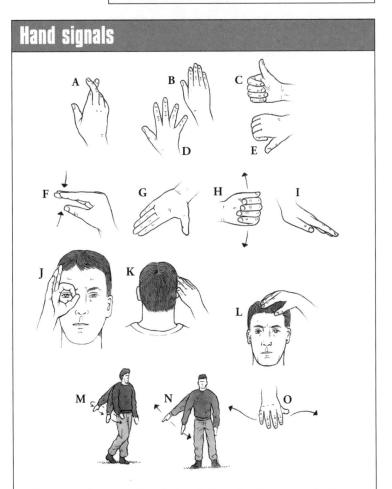

Military trackers use hand signals for silent communication. A – Track junction; B – Stop; C – Safe; D – Rest; E – Danger; F – Come close to talk; G – House; H – Hurry up; I – Slow down; J – Reconnaissance; K – Freeze and listen; L – Close on me; M – Turn around and go back; N – Move up; O – River or stream

CHAPTER TEN

Escape and Evasion

The skills that a tracker uses to pursue his quarry can also be used to advantage if the hunter becomes the hunted. Knowledge of tracking techniques will allow you to apply evasion tactics more effectively if the tables are turned on you.

Hopefully you will never have to deal with the situation of being taken captive; it is one of the most traumatic experiences, both physicaly and mentally, that anyone can undergo. This chapter is included more for general interest than practical instruction because anyone who really needs the following skills will probably have learned them in a special forces unit, and not from a book.

ESCAPE

Once you have been taken prisoner, your first priority will be to gather as much information as possible about where you are, in what kind of building or camp you are being detained, and how closely you are being guarded. Even if you have no idea how long you might be held for, begin planning and preparing for an escape as soon as you can.

Be aware that escape will not be easy without some kind of assistance. Most successful escapes are made through bribing a guard or with outside help. Breaking out, especially if you are alone, will be difficult.

GOING THROUGH A WALL

Check what the walls of your room or cell are made of. Old stone walls are probably sound, but an old brick wall or a breeze block wall, offer some hope if you can get hold of some sort of instrument – a spoon, pocket knife or even a piece of rock – with which you can scrape out the mortar. Check first to see which wall will be best to make a way through; if there is a choice of outside walls, pick the one with the best cover.

An old brick wall is the easiest to deal with. Your first objective, and the hardest and most time-consuming part of the process, should be to loosen one brick by removing all the mortar from around it. Choose a spot low on the wall that can be hidden by a bed or other furniture, and if it looks as if it is going to take several nights of work, disguise your handiwork by saving the powdered mortar, mixing it with saliva and pressing it back into the joint. Once you have removed a single brick, the neighbouring ones can be loosened much more quickly.

GOING OVER A FENCE

If there is a barbed wire perimeter fence to deal with, prepare yourself if possible by bringing a thick, doubled blanket or jacket (leather or canvas is best) with you. Tie the

Imprisonment

Begin planning an escape as soon as you have been captured, even if you do not know how long you may be held. It helps to keep up your morale.

corners or sleeves together and carry it around your shoulder like a cloak so that you can run and climb freely.

Climb to the top of the fence, hang on one-handed, and with the other hand pull the blanket over your head and fling it over the barbed wire above you. Use it to pull yourself up as high as possible then launch yourself over the top of the fence. The blanket or jacket will not provide complete protection from the barbs, but should make the process a little easier.

DIGGING A TUNNEL

Forget about it. this is the stuff of World War II escape films and is very unlikely to be a real option.

EVASION

Once you have made your escape, your captors are going to come looking for you. If you have good tracking skills, you can use them to your advantage in trying to evade the people searching for you. If you know for certain that your captors do not have a tracker of their own, then you are at a considerable advantage.

If they do possess a skilled tracker, then using the evasion techniques described below is not going to throw them off your trail, but your best chance is to lay false trails as a delaying tactic. Keep moving as quickly as possible, and you can hope to outstrip them.

In any escape situation, lead time – how far you are ahead of your pursuers – is by far the most important advantage you can have. Do everything you can to preserve it and, if possible, increase it. You can do this by:

● Delaying for as long as possible the time when your captors will discover that you have escaped
● Moving as quickly as possible
● Doing anything that will delay your pursuers, provided it does not slow you down too much.

You can put off the discovery of your escape in several ways, depending on where you have been imprisoned, and how you are being guarded. If guards check on you at regular intervals – whether this is every hour or once a day – plan your escape for the time immediately following an inspection.

Going through a wall

The hardest part of breaking through a wall is removing the first brick, which should be done with a knife. Once you have succeeded in loosening one brick, the rest are much easier.

Going over a fence

A fence topped by a roll of barbed wire or razor wire can be dealt with by slinging a leather jacket, piece of sacking or doubled, heavy blanket over it. Tie the sleeves or corners together so that you can 'wear' it like a cloak while you climb the chain-link fence below.

If they only look in on you occasionally at night, try to rig some sort of dummy that will make the guard think you are there sleeping. Think about this as soon as you arrive, and if possible sleep in a place and/or position that will make such a deception easier when the time actually comes to escape.

Once you have escaped, do not even think about hiding and waiting until your captors stop looking for you; the chances are that they will not, and you will have missed your best chance of getting away. Use whatever lead time you have to put as much distance between you and the enemy as possible. Only then should you begin to think about covering your trail and using certain deception tactics.

There are several standard deception tactics taught to sniper patrols and special forces units. However, these will all be well known to any experienced tracker, who will know how to spot them and will most likely be on the lookout for them. Trying to hide your trail takes time, and will allow an experienced tracker to gain on you. You will quickly have to weigh up whether the time you will gain by using deception techniques will outweigh the time you lose by putting them into operation.

BRUSHING YOUR TRACKS

Brushing your tracks is perhaps the oldest trick in the book, as seen in countless films. You use a leafy branch to brush your tracks away for a distance of several metres, or else cover them over with leaves, sand or earth, and then set off in a different direction.

Unfortunately, this trick is also one of the easiest ruses to spot. To a tracker, the brushing marks or the scattered leaves and soil are just as obvious a sign of his quarry as his footprints were. Perhaps worse, they actually tell the tracker that his quarry has tried to deceive him, so he will know to cast around for a new trail, possibly in a new direction.

WADING

Wading in a stream is another Hollywood favourite, but again it is neither as easy nor as effective as the movie world would have you believe. If the stream is shallow and clear, then you will leave behind sign on the stream bed for your pursuers to follow. Stones, gravel and bare rock on the bed of a stream become coated with a thin layer of algae that causes them to darken slightly; your passage will disturb this layer and create pale patches that are as clear to a tracker as any footprint.

In addition, walking or running in a stream, even a shallow one, is just plain slow. Wading knee deep is slower still, and swimming is not worth thinking about.

There is also the problem of where to leave the stream. Getting out of a stream or river without leaving obvious sign is practically impossible. On an easy, angled bank you will be dripping water everywhere, and on a steep one you will leave scuff mark, broken vegetation and footprints.

One of the few situations in which a stream or river can prove truly useful is when a fast-flowing stream is big enough to carry you in the direction you want to go. Of course, you will need one that flows faster than walking speed, is deep enough for you to float in, and that does not have dangerous rapids or waterfalls.

ROCK HOPPING

One of the most effective deception techniques is to walk on hard, rocky ground, or to hop from one rock to another in an area of boulders – at the edge of a river, for example. Of course, this requires that you find an area with sufficiently large boulders, spaced closely enough that you can jump from one to the next. If you try this on smaller stones, the stones will rock slightly under your weight leaving a slight gap around them that an experienced tracker will easily spot.

Even if the boulders are big enough not to move beneath your weight, you can still leave enough sign to allow a tracker to follow you. Any dirt on your footwear will be transferred to the first few rocks as faint smudges, so it is worth sitting down and cleaning the soles of your shoes, or even taking them off for a while if you can proceed without risking damage to your feet.

The further it is possible to travel on rock or stones, the better your chances of throwing off your pursuers, as following a track on this terrain can be slow and difficult work.

JUMPING OFF

As its name implies, this technique involves jumping sideways off your trail. If you are travelling alone, it should be used in conjunction with backtracking (see below), for the obvious reason that if your track just ends in the middle of nowhere, your tracker will know to look to one side or the other.

Jumping off is commonly used by military groups moving together. A few members will jump off and circle back to ambush the tracking party as they continue to follow the main trail. An astute tracker should, of course, be alert to any decrease in the density of the sign he is following and be immediately suspicious of a possible ambush.

BACKTRACKING

Walking backwards in your own footprints, or backtracking, is one of the few deception techniques you will see in the movies that is actually taught and used by the military. It is usually used in combination with jumping off, wading, or cutting the corner.

The footprints left by a person walking backwards are noticeably different from those left by some walking normally. When walking backward, your stride is shorter and more irregular, and your feet are usually further apart. The toe of the print will be deeper than normal, and soil will be displaced backwards, behind the heel, rather than forward of the toe.

Experiment by walking normally over a patch of soft ground, then taking a step or two to one side and walking backward beside your original track. Try walking backwards both slowly and as quickly as you can. Compare the various tracks and note the distinguishing features.

BACKTRACKING AND JUMPING OFF

This evasion tactic is best employed where there is good cover on either side of your route. Never begin backtracking just anywhere. If your tracks stop dead in the middle of a trail, your pursuers will immediately know that you are trying to deceive them. The idea is to make them waste time looking in the wrong places.

Choose a point where your tracks would become fainter or harder to follow – the edge of a stream or the beginning of a patch of hard or rocky ground – to begin your backtrack. That way, the tracker will not be immediately suspicious of the lack of sign.

Walk backwards carefully in your old footsteps for five to 10 paces to a place where you can jump off to one side. If possible, do this on the far side (from your pursuers' point of view) of a large tree or boulder, or some other form of cover, which will conceal your new trail from the view of those following.

If this tactic works, the tracking party will waste precious minutes casting around on the bank of the stream or on the hard ground looking for sign before suspecting a ruse and searching back along the sides of your trail. They will probably pick up your new track eventually, but you will have increased that vital lead time.

CUT-THE-CORNER

This is another standard military technique, which can be used as you approach a known road or trail. As you get close to the road, within 100m (300ft) or thereabouts, you alter your course about 45° to one side or the other – let's say to the right, in this example – and continue until you meet the road. Here you turn right and continue for a short distance, making sure you leave obvious signs that you are heading to the right (transferred soil if the road is asphalt, footprints if it is a dirt track).

Then you backtrack to the point where you joined the road and continue past it (having stamped all the dirt off your boots if it is an asphalt road, or making as little sign as possible if it is dirt) for the desired distance. You then leave the road on the far side and continue across country.

The aim of this deception is to make the trackers think that you saw the road up ahead and 'cut the corner' to the right, as that was your intended direction. Again, once they realize they have been tricked, they will waste valuable time casting around for your real trail.

SLIP-THE-STREAM

You can also use the cut-the-corner tactic at a stream or river. Approach the stream in the same manner, at a 45° angle, and wade a short distance upstream. Leave some false sign to make it look as if you have climbed out of the river and, if time permits, establish a false trail before backtracking into the water.

Backtracking

Walking backwards in your own footprints is one of the oldest tricks in the book, but it will only work if used carefully as part of a more sophisticated deception tactic.

Then follow the stream bed downstream for as far as you want, before leaving the water at a place of your choice and continuing your journey on land.

Always lay the false trail upstream and slip away downstream. If you try this the other way round, there is danger of silt and debris caused by your motion through the water being washed back down to the pursuing party and giving the game away.

LOOPING

Strictly speaking, this is not an evasion technique but a military tactic, and is of no use unless you are armed and willing to kill your pursuers. It is used by sniper patrols and special forces units when they suspect they are being followed.

Keep your eyes open for a possible vantage point off to one side of the route you are following. Once you have passed it, begin to alter your course off to that side, tightening the turn as you go until you have looped back and can climb up to your chosen point. You should now be in a position to watch and take stock of your pursuers. If the party is too large for your patrol to eliminate completely, you should at least get your best shot to take out the tracker before you move on.

TRACKER DOGS

The domestic dog is a distant cousin of the wolf, but thousands of years of domestication have not dulled its sense of smell. Dogs have relatively poor eyesight – they are largely colour blind, and cannot detect stationary creatures more than 50m (150ft) away – but possess very acute hearing and a highly developed sense of smell. This olfactory ability has been harnessed by the police and the military to help in searching for drugs, explosives and earthquake and avalanche victims, as well as for tracking fugitives.

It has been estimated that a dog's sense of smell is one million times more acute than that of a human, and far more sensitive than the best odour-detecting machines yet built. A tracker dog takes advantage of the fact that every human's sweat glands produce an odour that is as individual as a fingerprint. The dog can detect and follow minute traces of this odour where the quarry has touched or brushed against trees, rocks, or vegetation. It can also detect the odour in the air, where it has evaporated from the quarry, or his clothes, or from the objects he has touched.

Tracker dogs are usually accompanied by a human tracker, who checks the visual sign to make sure that the dog is following the desired quarry. A dog comes into its own where the quarry attempts any kind of deception tactic. Instead of the pursuit team having to cast around looking for the new trail, a dog will quickly find the track along which the quarry has disappeared.

This means that your evasion tactics will be different if you know that you are being tracked by dogs. There is no point wasting your own time on deception techniques – simply preserve your lead time and keep moving as fast as you can. An unleashed dog can maintain a speed of 13–16km/h (8–10mph) over open ground for several hours. Fortunately for the person being tracked, a tracker dog's speed will obviously be limited by the maximum speed of its handler, which is more likely to be around 6km/h (4mph).

EVADING TRACKER DOGS

First of all, be aware that hiding will not work – do not even consider it as an option. The dogs will find you. Attempting to hide up a tree will just end up with you trapped in the tree. Hiding in water is no better; the dog handler will quickly realize from his dog's behaviour that you are somewhere in the vicinity, and the search party will soon start checking all streams and water holes.

There are two main strategies to use when trying to escape from dogs – delaying your pursuers, and breaking the scent trail.

DELAYING TACTICS

There several ways of slowing up a dog and its handler:

● Climb over obstacles
● Walk on hard surfaces
● Walk along streams
● Get downwind if possible
● Pass through an area crowded with other people.

Climb over any walls or fences that will be difficult for a dog. High chainlink fences and deer fences are ideal. The handler will be slowed up considerably while he manhandles his dog over the obstruction.

Walking on a hard surface, especially in strong sunlight, leaves a weak scent trail that will rapidly dissipate in the heat. Asphalt roads, the tops of walls, bare rocky ground and sun-baked earth are all good surfaces to choose.

Although a dog will always be able to pick up your scent wherever you exit from the water, taking to a stream will slow up the search party a little, as the dog casts up and down the bank looking for your trail.

Always try to work your way downwind of the search party, as it will make the dog's task harder, especially if you can combine this tactic with the hard-surface ploy mentioned previously. If you can afford to show yourself, then it may be possible to throw off the dogs by passing through an area which is loaded with the scent of many other human beings, such as a crowded street or market place.

Tracker dogs

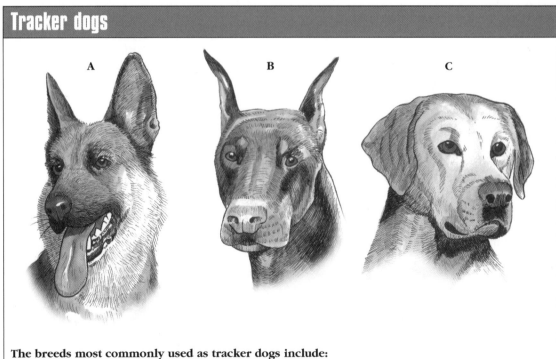

The breeds most commonly used as tracker dogs include:
A – Alsatians or German Shepherds; B – Dobermanns; C – Labradors

Tracker teams

A tracker team usually consists of several tracker dogs with their handlers, led by an experienced human tracker who evaluates the visual sign left by the quarry.

BREAKING THE SCENT TRAIL

In trying to break a scent trail, factors that work in your favour include:

● Time
● Hard, stony ground without vegetation
● A wind blowing in your direction of travel
● Heavy rain
● Strong, hot sun.

Factors which work against you include:

● Long grass and undergrowth
● A wind blowing against your direction of travel
● Mild, overcast conditions.

A scent trail will eventually dissipate with time, so anything you can do to delay discovery and the onset of a tracker dog search will help. In average conditions, a scent trail can evaporate and 'go cold' in around eight hours.

Traces of your scent will stick to just about everything touched by you or your clothes, so long grass and vegetation make for a good scent trail. A trail over hard, stony ground with sparse vegetation is more difficult for a dog to follow unless there is also airborne scent to guide it. You can tell when a tracker dog finds the ground trail growing faint – it raises its head and sniffs the breeze.

In addition to the scent traces you leave on the ground and vegetation, your odour is continually dispersing into the air around you and being carried away on the breeze. If you can stay well downwind of a tracker dog there is little chance that it will pick up your airborne scent.

Other meteorological factors that play to your advantage are heavy rain, which can help to wash away a ground trail, and hot sun, which increases the evaporation rate of the ground scent, speeding the dispersal of the scent. However, hot sun will make you sweat more, increasing the strength of your airborne trail.

The ultimate way to break a scent trail is to steal a horse, bicycle or vehicle, though you will have to weigh the advantages against the increased possibility of being discovered.

MASKING YOUR SCENT

There are very few substances that will effectively mask the scent of a human being to the extent that a dog will be put off the trail.

Diesel and lubricating oil, garlic and aniseed can be useful in masking your wind-blown scent, if placed across your trail upwind of the dogs.

However, do not try to hide your scent by applying a masking agent to your clothing or body. This will just add another component to your own smell, and will not affect a dog's ability to follow your trail.

DECOY SCENT

A decoy is some strong-smelling object that you drag along behind you in the hope that its scent will overpower your own. If you then choose a good spot to discard the decoy – at a point where you can take to water or continue along a road or railway for some distance – there is a good chance that you will be able to break your scent trail. Of course, this is only worth trying in windless conditions or if you are heading downwind, otherwise the dogs could pick up your airborne trail.

Unfortunately, the only object you are likely to come across in the country-side that will have a power-ful enough stink is the decomposing corpse of a dead animal – unpleasant but effective. Drag it on a short length of rope or string, and make sure not to touch the corpse while you are tying it on in case its scent sticks to your hands.

REPELLENTS

There are commercial sprays that are designed to repel male dogs – their main pur-pose is to deter stray males from approaching a bitch in heat. They are meant to work by presenting an odour that a dog will find extremely unpleas-ant, but in the field it has been shown that a well-trained tracker dog will still hunt down a quarry tainted with a repellent spray.

FENDING OFF DOG ATTACKS

Tracker dogs are often backed up by attack dogs. Do not underestimate the power of an attack dog; they can easily kill an adult human. A dog can bite down with a force of around 165kg (360lb); a human bite is a max-imum of 29kg (64lb) force.

An attack by a single dog can usually be dealt with if you are armed with a knife or a heavy rock. The dog will have been trained to go for your arm, groin or throat. Stay low and strike upward. If you are alone and faced by two or more dogs, never try to take them on. Get away if possible and do everything you can to avoid an attack.

Dog attack

Prepare for a dog attack by rolling some form of protection (a jacket or heavy cloth) around your forearm. Offer the dog your arm as it comes at you; the protection should buy you enough time to eliminate the dog with a knife or heavy object.

Glossary

altimeter - an instrument that measures altitude, or height above a certain point (usually sea level).

bearing - the compass direction from your position to a landmark or destination.

back bearing - the compass direction from a landmark to your position.

chart - a map used for navigation at sea or in an aircraft.

collecting feature - a linear feature in the landscape that allows you to maintain your direction of travel without reference to the compass.

contour - a line on a map joining points of equal elevation.

convergence - the difference in degrees between true north and grid north at any given place.

coordinates - a pair of numbers and/or letters that describe a unique position

course - the route or path between two points.

datum - a reference point used by cartographers, from which all elevations or positions on a map or chart are measured.

declination - the difference in degrees between true north and magnetic north at any given place.

degree - the unit of measurement of an angle. A full circle is divided into 360 degrees; each degree is divided into 60 minutes, and each minute into 60 seconds.

deviation - any error introduced into a compass reading by the presence of nearby iron or steel objects, magnets or electrical currents.

direct bearing - the compass direction from your position to a landmark.

easting - a position's distance east or west of a given reference line. The longitude of a position (ie its distance east or west of the Greenwich meridian) is an example of an easting. See also northing.

elevation - height above mean sea level.

equinox - one of two points in the earth's orbit when everywhere on earth experiences 12 hours of darkness and 12 hours of daylight.

GMT - Greenwich Mean Time, the time as measured at Greenwich Observatory in London, UK (longitude 0°); also known as Universal Time (see also UTC).

grid - the horizontal and vertical lines on a map that allow you to describe position.

grid north - north defined in relation to a cartographic grid.

grid reference - a position defined in relation to a cartographic grid.

handrail - a linear feature in the landscape that you can use to keep track of the direction in which you are heading.

heading - the compass direction in which you are moving.

hyperthermia - a condition in which the body temperature rises to a dangerously high level. Also known as heatstroke.

hypothermia - a condition in which the body temperature falls to a dangerously low level. Also known as exposure.

imperial mile – the standard measurement of distance on land in the United Kingdom and the USA. It is equal to 1.609km or 1760 yards.

kilometre – the standard measurement of distance on land throughout most of the world. It is equal to 1000 metres, or 0.621 imperial miles.

latitude – a measure of distance north or south of the equator.

log – an instrument used for measuring the speed of a boat.

longitude – a measure of distance east or west of the prime meridian.

magnetic north – the direction of the magnetic north pole.

meridian – an imaginary line joining points of equal longitude, running from pole to pole on the earth's surface.

nautical mile – the standard measurement of distance used by marine navigators. It is equal to one minute of longitude, or 1.852km 1.151 or imperial miles.

northing – a position's distance north or south of a given reference line. The latitude of a position (ie its distance north or south of the Equator) is an example of a northing. See also easting.

pedometer – an instrument that measures the distance you have walked.

position line – a line along which you know your position must lie, for example a compass bearing of a landmark, or a transit.

prime meridian – the line of longitude that passes through Greenwich in London, also known as the Greenwich meridian.

projection – a mathematical method of representing the three-dimensional surface of the earth on a two-dimensional map or chart.

quarry – in tracking, the animal or human that is being hunted or pursued.

resection – the method of fixing your position by taking two or more compass bearings of landmarks and plotting the point on

the map where they intersect.

romer – a graduated scale marked on the transparent baseplate of a compass that allows the user to read grid references from the map quickly and easily.

satellite geometry – the arrangement of satellites in the sky above a GPS receiver as it tries to compute its position.

sign – any physical indication of the passage of an animal or human quarry. A footprint is the most obvious example of sign.

spring tide – spring tides occur every 14 days or so, just after new moon and full moon. At these times the tidal range (ie the difference in height between low tide and high tide) is at its greatest.

stalking – in tracking, the art of moving silently and stealthily so as not to alert the quarry to your presence.

tidal stream – a horizontal current caused by the rise or fall of the tide.

track – a line of sign that indicates the route of an animal or human quarry through the environment.

tracking – the pursuit of an animal or human quarry by observing and following the sign that they have left behind. See also sign.

trailing – another word for tracking.

transit – an imaginary straight line extended through two landmarks and used as a position line.

true north – the direction of the geographic north pole.

UTC – Universal Time Coordinated. The same as Greenwich Mean Time (GMT). Used as a universal time constant in navigation; GPS satellites and receivers operate on UTC.

UTM grid – Universal Transverse Mercator grid. A grid reference system that covers the globe and is used on many maps throughout the world.

waypoint – a particular, user-specified location along a route. GPS receivers follow a winding course by navigating from one waypoint to the next.

index

References in italics refer to illustration captions